JENNIFER, LIAM and JOSH

JENNIFER, LIAM and JOSH

An Unauthorized Biography of the Stars of the

HUNGER GAMES

DANNY WHITE

First published in Great Britain in 2013 by
Michael O'Mara Books Limited
9 Lion Yard
Tremadoc Road
London SW4 7NQ

A CIP catalogue record for this book is available from the British Library.

Papers used by Michael O'Mara Books Limited are natural, recyclable
products made from wood grown in sustainable forests. The
manufacturing processes conform to the environmental regulations of the
country of origin.

ISBN: 978-1-78243-173-2 in hardback print format
ISBN: 978-1-78243-182-4 in trade paperback format
ISBN: 978-1-78243-184-8 in e-book format

1 2 3 4 5 6 7 8 9 10

Designed and typeset by Design 23
Jacket design by Ana Bjezancevic

Printed and bound by CPI Group (UK) Ltd, Croydon, CR0 4YY

www.mombooks.com

PART ONE

LIFE BEFORE THE GAMES

Chapter One

JENNIFER:
COUNTRY LIFE

With the benefit of hindsight, it is clear that the hand of destiny that guided Jennifer Lawrence to the role of Katniss Everdeen in *The Hunger Games* can be seen throughout the events of her childhood and her subsequent meteoric rise in the film industry. The rebellious child of twenty-first-century cinema, she instinctively challenges many of the industry's rules and regulations, particularly some of the more proscriptive ones that apply to females. If this means that some do not look on her with affection, well, that is fine with her: 'I'm just not likeable all the time,' she has said. Jennifer has a confidence and wisdom beyond her years, and she believes that this is something with which she was born. 'I have an old soul,' she told *Interview* magazine. Likeable or not, her wise, assured nature has helped her land one of this century's most sought-after female movie roles, making her the toast of Hollywood. Yet her childhood was far from glittering.

Jennifer Shrader Lawrence was born into a changing world on 15 August 1990. In the year of her birth, Germany was reunified, Nelson Mandela was released from jail in South Africa, America went to war with Iraq over Saddam Hussein's occupation of Kuwait and the Internet was invented. The movie world was also changing, with CGI techniques advancing in one of the year's biggest releases, *Total Recall*. Among other films to draw the crowds that year were *Ghost*, *Pretty Woman*, *Dances with Wolves* and *Home Alone*. The showbiz year ended with Tom Cruise marrying actress Nicole Kidman on Christmas Eve.

Meanwhile, Jennifer was taking her first breaths in the outside world, as her family adapted to the new arrival. Jennifer told the *Belfast Telegraph*: 'I grew up in such a normal family.' She realized, though, that this statement would need clarification. 'OK, we weren't that normal – I had a goat for a pet – but we were semi-normal.' Her parents had met during their higher education. Her mother Karen was born in 1956 and attended Westport High School in Westport, California. After graduating in 1974, she went to the University of Louisville in Kentucky. It was there she met Gary, Jennifer's father.

By the time Jennifer came along, Gary owned a construction company called Lawrence and Associates INC, while Karen ran a children's day camp called Camp Hi-Ho – 'where kids come first'. The camp promises prospective visitors 'summer fun for Louisville, KY area kids 5–13 years old'. As the website states: 'Children can catch a fish, swim, ride horses, paddle boats and canoes, snuggle up with puppies and kittens, play sports, shoot water guns in the tree fort, swing on a rope swing, speed down a zip line, show off skills at the talent show, cool off on the 100-foot slip 'n' slide, lather up in the shaving cream "war", bounce off the BLOB into the lake, get a face paint, tie-dye a shirt and catch critters!' Eventually, Gary stepped aside from his construction duties to help Karen with her growing project.

Their first two children were both male, and Jennifer was an unplanned addition to the clan. 'We thought we were finished having kids,' her mother told *Rolling Stone*. 'We got rid of the baby bed and everything.' They nicknamed their daughter 'Plays With Fire'; it was only later in life that Jennifer realized they chose this name to reflect the fact that they had played with fire and, in the form of an unexpected pregnancy, got their fingers burned. This was not her only moniker: she was also nicknamed 'Nitro', which means hyper. Her two older brothers are called Ben and Blaine.

Jennifer stood out from the start: she was in fact the first female to be born on the Lawrence side of the family for over fifty years. Although Karen has spoken of her excitement at the arrival of a daughter, saying, 'I couldn't wait to have a little girl and dress her up,' Jennifer soon showed that she had her own ideas about her attire. She preferred to wear jeans and sweaters, just like her big brothers. This would influence her upbringing enormously: the family were keen that she was not overindulged into 'little princess' territory, so they sometimes overcompensated, treating her robustly rather than with kid gloves. As she told *Elle* magazine, Jennifer is now aware that her family were so adamant that she would not turn into a princess that they 'went in the exact opposite direction'. Her mother agrees: 'I didn't want her to be a diva,' said Karen. 'I didn't mind if she was girlie, as long as she was tough.'

One day, while in pre-school, this came to a head when Jennifer was banned from playing with other girls, due to her unruly nature. 'She didn't mean to hurt them,' her mum told *Rolling Stone*. 'They were just making cookies, and she wanted to play ball.' A neighbour of the family saw a different side to the youngster. Speaking to the *New York Daily News*, Jane Schmidt described the Lawrence clan as 'a wonderful Christian family', and Jennifer as 'very sweet'.

But behind the doors of the household things were often boisterous. For instance, when Jennifer once slapped one of her brothers on the arm, he threw her down the stairs in response. 'Can we talk about excessive force, please?' she asked him. Those moments hurt at the time, but prepared her well for her future existence as, in the words of *Rolling Stone* magazine, 'America's kick-ass sweetheart'. The months of intensive training she had to undergo for *The Hunger Games* bordered on brutal at times. Her experience of rough-and-tumble in her formative years served her well in other ways, too. For instance, she communicates confidently with men thanks to growing up with two male siblings. 'I grew up with brothers so I normally talk to guys like boys talk to boys,' she told *The Sun*.

But growing up as the younger sibling of two brothers, the experience of 'Jen', as the family knew her, was different to that of Katniss Everdeen. As the youngest sibling in the family, she will have been prone to certain characteristics, according to those who subscribe to the theory that a child's 'birth order' has a significant influence on their development. For instance, she would be likely to be outgoing and charming, with a tendency for manipulation. She would also be expected to be single-minded, determined and rebellious, and certainly not one to pay much heed to accepted norms or rules. Youngest siblings are, according to the theories outlined by author Linda Blair in her book *Birth Order*, happy to take risks. However, Blair also argues that when the first child of a gender is born, parents sometimes treat that child more as a firstborn, such is their excitement over the new arrival. This tendency magnifies in families with three or more children. A personality-based school of thought that Lawrence does subscribe to is astrology: she describes herself as a 'fiery Leo'. She has demonstrated several of the star sign's characteristics, including confidence, creativity and ambition. But then, most successful actors have done so – and not all of them are Leos. However, her identification with her sign forms another part of her self-definition.

The family lived on a farm in Shelby County, in the state of Kentucky. The county, which is named after the first governor of Kentucky Isaac Shelby, has a wholesome tradition: its motto is 'good land, good living, good people'. As for Kentucky itself, it is known as the 'Bluegrass State', a nickname it earned because of the form of grass its fertile soil encourages. It is also known for bluegrass music, its high number of deer and turkeys, horse racing, tobacco and bourbon whiskey. If all this sounds a bit male, then that helps further explain Jennifer's tomboy nature. Both inside and outside the house, there were plenty of masculine influences. With her looks somewhat resembling those of Bond girl actress Ursula Andress, and with her smoky, husky voice and no-nonsense determination in life, she is very much a child of Kentucky. She liked the area – and still does. 'She is a Louisvillian at heart,' her brother Ben Lawrence told the *Daily News*. He added that her appeal comes through her authenticity – something that was part of her make-up from the start. 'She is just a bad liar,' he said. 'She has to be honest.'

It was only when, years later, Jennifer was talking to a friend in California about their respective childhoods that she realized how much her Kentucky upbringing had influenced her. 'I was like, "You never had any woods, you never dug a hole, or saw a snake, or climbed a tree?"' she recalled to *The Sun*. 'She was like, "Well, I had the beach," and I said, "But where did you fall out of trees? Where did you build your forts?"' Jennifer pitied her friend, as she herself so loved the great outdoors and wildlife. Her first horse was a pony named Muffin: 'She was cute,' she recalled to *Rolling*

Stone, 'but she was a mean little bitch.' She went on to add three more ponies to her collection. First came two males called Dan and Brumby. 'Those two hated each other, but then one day there was a big storm and they spent the night huddled in the barn together, and suddenly they were inseparable,' she said. 'The sexual tension finally boiled over.' Then came another pony called Brandy. 'So white-trash,' she said. 'That was during my tube-top phase.' Amid all this outdoor, natural living, Jennifer's was not a childhood drenched in culture. She told *Seventeen* magazine that she 'didn't grow up in an artistic house', and admitted apologetically that she grew up watching unchallenging, mainstream films – 'things like *Home Alone*.'

One person who remembers her love of nature from those days is her childhood friend Spencer Jenkins. He describes her as a 'lanky, tall tomboy with the most outrageous personality ever.' Writing in the *Sentinel News*, he declared: 'If I could sum her up in one word, it would simply be funny . . . with awkward as a close second.' Jenkins met Jennifer through his friend Carrie Miller, who is Jennifer's cousin. His parents had known Gary and Karen during their respective schooldays. Karen had been a significant source of support when Jenkins's father was diagnosed with cancer. Desipte her many commitments, she visited him right up until he passed away in 2010.

As for Jennifer herself, Jenkins has warm memories of carefree childhood days at the Miller family's pony farm in Middletown, driving around in their Gator vehicle, which they overloaded with youngsters, including their friend Carrie. They would, Jenkins told *Sentinel News*, drive 'aimlessly and recklessly' around the grounds. 'Jen and Carrie liked to have fun and weren't afraid to get dirty when we were driving through the mud on the Gator,' he added. At weekends, Jennifer and the gang would 'take our romper room attitudes to the Lyndon YMCA.' Jenkins continued: 'During the nights that it was set up for kids, we'd dance, eat and of course hit the huge obstacle course, Play Land. We would run through that course, and the rest of the Y, until we collapsed from laughter and pure exhaustion.' Jenkins says Jennifer was, back then, what she is now: a 'tough, athletic girl with a strong personality'. Jennifer just remembers loving visiting the farm. 'I went there almost every day,' she recalls. 'My brothers were into fishing, but I was all about the horses.'

Jennifer also helped out at her mother's day camp. Ever the tomboy, she led fun-packed games of softball and field hockey. As indefatigable as she was enthusiastic, she also offered spontaneous cheerleading classes to some of the girls, who gleefully joined in. These moments gave her a connection with others that she often lacked at school. 'I changed schools a lot when ·I was in elementary school because some girls were mean,' she told *The Sun*. 'They were less mean in middle school, because I was doing all right, although this one girl gave me invitations to hand out to her birthday party that I wasn't invited to. But that was fine, I just . . . threw them in the trashcan.'

That girl, called Meredith, has left quite an impression on Jennifer. At the time of the incident, Jennifer tried to take the proverbial high road by deciding that, when she herself had her next birthday party, she would invite Meredith despite the callous omission. 'So I won,' said Jennifer, lending even a moment of grace an edge of competition, all the better to characteristically shroud the vulnerability of it all. 'Even the Nazis didn't do what they did simply to be evil,' she added of Meredith. 'I'm so happy I'm comparing Meredith to a Nazi,' she continued, throwing all caution to the wind. 'I hope she reads this.'

She did encounter happier times and meet nicer people during her schooldays, though. She attended Kammerer Middle School, and while there she met a boy called Andy Strunk, who had Down's syndrome. She was a supportive friend to Andy, as his mother Pollyanna Strunk recalled in an interview with *New York Daily News*. 'She always had a soft heart for him,' she said. 'She always looked out for him. Middle school is a tough place to be, especially for a kid with special needs.' Having been voted by her classmates as the 'most talkative' pupil, Jennifer helped Andy run for the position of 'Mr Kammerer'. 'It's like king for the day,' Pollyanna explained. 'She nominated him, and he won. She would talk to her friends and tell them to vote for him. She is very charismatic. It's just her natural person coming out.' As for Strunk himself, he says: 'She's kind . . . I think she has spirit.' She was also a cheerleader for a while and once performed one of the chants she had belted out in her childhood for a *Rolling Stone* interviewer. 'Ain't, no, sweat! [clap] This game ain't over yet! [clap],' went the rendition.

Among other happy memories she recalls an eighth-grade school project she embarked upon that caused quite a shock wave. 'I did a science experiment in eighth grade that almost shut down my school,' she told *Rolling Stone*. 'I had this theory that hand-washing is overrated. And it was true: the bathroom door had the same bacteria as the toilet seat, and the sink was the dirtiest part – it was dirtier than the toilet handle! It had disgusting amounts.' To this day, she remains of the opinion that the most hygienic thing may be to not wash your hands after lavatory breaks. She was interested in such matters as a child when, for a while, she wanted to be a doctor. Another passing ambition she had was to become a travel agent.

However, her energetic and rebellious nature led to her feeling stifled at school, and pushed her towards a more artistic career path. She recalls being ticked off by a maths teacher for not understanding what was being taught in class. 'I always felt dumber than everybody else,' Lawrence told the *Los Angeles Times*. 'I hated it. I hated being inside. I hated being behind a desk. School just kind of killed me.' She began to dream of a more exciting and liberating life. In time, she became clearer on how she could achieve such a life.

Fortunately, or not, depending on how you look at it, as Jennifer began to dream of becoming an actress, she did not have to contend with pressure from 'pushy' or 'stage' parents. In fact, she said, they were the 'exact opposite' of that. 'They did everything in their power to keep it from happening,' she told *Hello!* magazine. Although this is something of an exaggeration, much like some of the heroines she would go on to portray on the big screen, Jennifer was not one to be held back. As she turned fourteen, she had made up her mind: she wanted to become an actress. It would take a brave person to try and stop her.

As she embarked on the 'getting serious' part of the process, she had minimal experience under her belt. At the age of nine she had trodden some very amateur boards when she appeared in a local church production based on the biblical Book of Jonah. Her part was as a prostitute from Nineveh. Karen says her daughter was the star turn of the production. 'The other girls just stood there with lipstick on,' she told *Rolling Stone*, 'but she came in swinging her booty and strutting her stuff.' Afterwards, friends of the family approached Karen with some eccentric praise. 'We don't know if we should congratulate you or not, because your kid's a great prostitute,' they told her.

This was not necessarily the sort of praise to alleviate her parents' concerns about Jennifer's dream, but they supported their daughter as best they could. Her first breaks came after she was brought to the attention of two New York talent agencies. She auditioned at the first agency's headquarters, after convincing Karen to take her to Manhattan. To her delight, they told Jennifer that it was the best 'cold read' they had ever heard from a fourteen-year-old. Karen, ever the cautious presence, warned her daughter that they might say that to all the girls. Yet, as fate would have it, another agent spotted Jennifer in the Manhattan streets on the same day. She and Karen had paused to watch some break-dancers strutting their stuff on Union Square when the agent noticed the teenager. He was busy shooting a commercial for the H&M clothing chain, and when he saw Jennifer he saw dollar signs. He asked if he could take her photograph and then offered her a series of advertising and modelling deals.

'It wasn't creepy, he didn't ask to take me anywhere, he just wanted to take a picture,' Jennifer told the *New York Daily News*, mindful of the conclusions many would draw from the episode. But she was not interested in modelling, however flattering the attention was for her. 'I was offered a number of modelling contracts soon after but turned them down,' she told the *Daily Telegraph*. 'I was like, "Actually, I think I'm going to be an actor." That was an incredibly dumb thing to do at fourteen but was probably the one time when my self-assuredness paid off.' Many girls her age would have wilted under the sheer flattery of being told they could model. Not Jennifer – she kept her eyes focused on her real passion: acting. She wanted to appear in films that would be shown in the huge cinemas in Manhattan's Times Square.

Meanwhile, her mother and father still had their own ideas over what their precious daughter's immediate future should look like. They insisted that she must complete her high school education before pursuing her acting career properly. They wanted her to have all the usual options open to her if her dream did not come true. Despite her impatience to get on with chasing her dream, Jennifer accepted the deal and knuckled down hard to graduate, which she did with a 3.9 average. To be clear, though, she did not buy into her parents' fear that she would not succeed as an actor. 'I never considered that,' she said. She told *Hello!* that the thought '. . . if it doesn't work out' simply 'never popped into [her] mind'. Looking back, she sees this as the 'dumb determination' of a 'naïve fourteen-year-old'.

Her regular deployment of the 'dumb' word to describe her teenage confidence is at once self-deprecating and boastful. Her determination served her well as she moved to New York, the city that never sleeps. Its energy, cultural richness and the sheer ambition that is exuded by its towering buildings all appealed to Jennifer and spoke to her mood as she arrived there with Karen in 2006. Her quest was, in her eyes, mission possible. Fuelling her determination was the scepticism of her friends back in Kentucky. She felt they were waiting for her to fail. 'I was like, "I'll show you,"' she said. And she did.

Chapter Two

JENNIFER:
FIRST BREAKS

Far from arriving as another intimidated visitor to the Big Apple, Jennifer simply walked in like she owned the place. 'My feet hit the pavement and you'd have thought I was born and raised there,' she said in *Beyond District 12*. 'I took over that town.' However, her father back home did not share her enthusiasm. Throughout Jennifer and Karen's first year in New York, he wanted them to return to Kentucky. This caused a lot of tension between her parents. 'That was a rough time,' Jennifer told a fan site. 'It was the first time I heard them fight.'

Typically for her, she used the tension as yet further motivation to succeed. Once she landed her big part, she told herself, she could at least make all the heartache and disruption worthwhile. Yet as she went for more and more cold readings, she feared that she would begin to bore her mother, as all she could talk about was her 'obsession'. Her first break came in an advertisement for the MTV series *My Super Sweet 16*. She played a spoilt girl called Lisa on her birthday. In the opening of the ad, she is carried into her party by a group of men who accidentally drop her. In the second scene she is about to blow out the candles on her birthday cake when a mirror ball crashes from the ceiling, covering her and the guests in cake.

The most significant factor in her taking this small, promotional part was that it earned her the right to a much-coveted card from the Screen Actors Guild. Speaking at an SAG ceremony later in life, she looked back at the symbolic and practical significance of his. 'I earned my SAG card when I was fourteen,' she said. 'I remember getting it in the mail and it being the best day in my entire life because it officially made me a professional actor, which put me in a category with all of you.' Following the *Super Sweet* slot came roles in advertisements for a range of firms including Verizon Wireless and Burger King, as she took her first, tentative steps in the industry.

What she wanted, though, was what she would consider a genuine acting role; she set herself high standards. Ultimately, she wanted to appear on the big screen, but she understood that television was her most likely point of entry. Her suspicions proved correct as she successfully auditioned for a part in a US television comedy called *The Bill Engvall Show*. Set in suburban Louisville, Colorado, the sitcom followed the fortunes of a counsellor called Bill Pearson and his family. Jennifer appeared as the eldest of the family's children. Her portrayal of Lauren, who was always at the centre of any family mischief, was a hit. In 2008, she won a Young Artist Award for Outstanding Young Performer in a TV Series – her first gong.

The pay cheque for the show was handsome, but for Jennifer the biggest significance of that was not anything materialistic or greedy, more that it bought her the freedom to be more discerning with future decisions. For that reason, she told *Seventeen* magazine, taking the part 'was one of the best decisions I ever made.' She explained 'I don't think at sixteen I really had the mindset of, "If I do that then I'll be able to do this", I just think it happened that way; but, yes, that show meant I could afford to turn down the crap movies and do what I loved.'

That same year came the moment she had been waiting for: her first film role. As well as *The Bill Engvall Show*, she had appeared in other television programmes including *Monk*, *Medium*, *Cold Case* and *Company Town*. However, it was her part in the film *Garden Party*, playing a character called Tiff, which was most significant in her career path as it took her into cinemas. That said, it was a brief part, in which she sits with two other sultry female teenagers smoking in a cafe. She had finally proved to herself, her parents and to all the doubters back home that she could do it.

She barely had time to celebrate, though, as having secured her first film role, two more came along in swift succession. Her part in *The Burning Plain* was a key role. She played Mariana, the daughter of Kim Basinger's character Gina. Mariana accidentally kills Gina and her lover Nick, before starting a fling with Nick's son. In an action-packed plot, Mariana falls pregnant, flees across the border into Mexico, and ultimately cuts all her ties, disappearing into the night for a new life under the new identity of Sylvia. the *Daily Telegraph* wrote that the gritty film had 'all the right credentials: it is serious-minded and dramatic, with universal themes and a clutch of fine acting performances'. Wendy Ide, writing for *The Times*, described it as an 'elegantly structured tale of lives laced together with tragedy and guilt'. In the wake of the film, Jennifer collected the second award of her career, winning the Marcello Mastroianni Award for Best Young Emerging Actor/Actress at the Venice Film Festival. If the award itself was thrilling, more exciting was the fact that in order to receive it she and her family embarked upon their first ever trip to Europe. 'We went for two weeks before and travelled around,' she said. 'That was so fun.' As she looked at Venice's gondolas and canals, she felt both vindicated and excited.

She also took a part in a film called *The Poker House* – and again she would emerge with an industry award to her name. Here, she played Agnes, a teenage girl living with her two sisters in her mother's whorehouse and gambling den. In one scene in the dark film, Agnes is raped by her mother's pimp, who suggests that she, too, should become a prostitute. It had been a harrowing experience at times to play the role, yet she was rewarded with the Outstanding Performance Award at the Los Angeles Film Festival. *LA Weekly* described the film as 'one of the most personal, wounded films in years', while *Movie Metropolis* prophetically concluded: 'Ms Lawrence is so persuasive we must mark her as a rising star.'

Just two years after moving to Manhattan in search of a dream, Jennifer was already living it and being recognized by key award ceremonies and the reviewing community. Far from peaking too soon, she was just getting started. Next up came a role that she wanted so badly that she would, she says, 'have walked on hot coals' to land it. From the moment she completed her first reading of the script for *Winter's Bone*, she decided that Ree Dolly was the best female role she had ever studied. She related instinctively to Ree's 'tenacity'. For the audition she aimed to look 'as ugly as possible'. She did not wash her hair for a week beforehand and wore no make-up on the day. 'I looked beat up in there,' she said. One cannot help feeling that Ree herself would have appreciated the approach Jennifer took to land the right to play her.

'It wasn't a fun, easy movie to make by any means,' says Jennifer. 'But I didn't do it to have fun.' She was exposed to a great deal of poverty as the film was shot in gritty locations, but insisted that she 'never felt sorry' for the needy folk she encountered. Instead, she reversed the roles and looked at wealthy America through their eyes. She wondered if they would feel sorry for the better-off, because many comfortable people had poorer family lives than those struggling with poverty. It is a creative, if somewhat flawed, perspective on it. But there is a very Jennifer-esque honesty to it: many Hollywood stars would have choked back tears while telling an interviewer how the poverty they saw 'broke their hearts' . . . before ordering another poolside cocktail.

Jennifer was taught how to chop wood for the film, but learning how to skin a squirrel was one of the more hair-raising tasks she had to undertake. During an interview she flippantly referred to the People for the Ethical Treatment of Animals (PETA) lobby group. 'I should say [the squirrel] wasn't real, for PETA – but screw PETA.' She added that she was 'okay with blood and guts'. Another challenge came in the scenes in which she was hunting with a shotgun. For these, she called on a relative who owned such a weapon. She would carry the gun around her cousin's house, simply to become more convincing in the way she held it. 'I wanted to be practised,' said Jennifer.

Winter's Bone sees Jennifer again play the role of the eldest sibling in a dysfunctional family. Ree's catatonic mother has been abandoned by Ree's meth addict father. Ree does her best to care for her mother and her two younger siblings at the family's home in southern Missouri. That home comes under threat when the family learns that the absent father had promised the house as part of a bond, so if he does not appear for an imminent court date the family will be evicted. Ree then enters her father's dark world in order to track him down.

Jennifer knew that to viewers the part would look challenging, and in many ways it was. But it was not the emotionally draining experience that some might suspect: 'I don't invest any of my real emotions,' she said, forever fronting her hard exterior to the world, despite the vulnerabilities that must hide secretly underneath.

The *Daily Telegraph* described her as 'old beyond

her years' and her performance as 'shocking'. *The Guardian* said: 'Lawrence is excellent as Ree: intelligent, and possessed of a moral courage that commands respect.' The praise just kept on coming as *Empire* marvelled, 'Lawrence's indomitable performance as a young woman pushed to breaking point by the desire to remain loyal to local customs and the will to survive is a truly standout piece of work.' *The Independent* slightly strangely said Jennifer resembled a younger Renée Zellweger, but was on the mark with its assessment of her performance, saying that in her 'unflinching blue eyes and wide cheekbones we discern a self-command absolutely right for her character'.

By now, Jennifer had a strong record of winning awards for projects she undertook. Yet with *Winter's Bone* she took a massive leap upwards when she was nominated for Best Actress at the Golden Globes and Oscars. She became the second-youngest nominee in the history of the Oscars, and she could afford to be optimistic, as *Winter's Bone* picked up several gongs at other award ceremonies. Not that you would ever catch her admitting to any optimism. Like most actors in such a position, she played the whole thing down. So did Karen, telling the media that her daughter never even mentioned the nomination herself and had asked her not to raise it either. 'I'm sure she'd be thrilled and honoured, but there are just some heavy hitters in her category.'

Indeed, Jennifer even went as far as quips that she would be disappointed if she won, as that would steal from her the opportunity to perform her 'losing face', which she said she had rehearsed carefully. She also insisted that she was excited about the fact that one of her favourite bands, Florence and the Machine, were to perform at the Oscars ceremony. On the night itself, she again bucked the Hollywood trend by ignoring a suggestion from a stylist that she confine herself to a small salad ahead of the red carpet: 'I said, "I'm getting a Philly cheesesteak,"' she recalled to the *New York Daily News*. Having negotiated the big arrival and posing for the army of snappers, she took her seat in the arena itself. She sat next to her father, his doubts over the move to New York now long gone. Instead, he and his daughter kept gazing over at each other, as if to say: 'I can't believe this is happening!'

The Best Actress gong did not go her way at either ceremony, instead it was handed to Natalie Portman for her performance in the much-discussed ballet film *Black Swan*. At least Jennifer got to perform her 'disappointed face'. Karen said that what mattered to her was not awards but the reputation her daughter had among the cast and crew of the films she had starred in. The mother was beyond proud when Jennifer's colleagues told her how 'gracious' and 'down-to-earth' she was. The girl herself said that while recognition and parties were great, what really made her happy was that she had found a way of being paid to do something she really loved doing. She felt excited that she could do this every day of her life.

Much as she loves working in the movie world, Jennifer remains revolted by several of that world's unwritten rules. Her rebellious side simmers over, for instance, when she thinks about some of the pressures put on famous women regarding their appearance. She says, for instance, that she is 'sick' of women being expected to have the figure of a 'prepubescent thirteen-year-old boy'. Instead of chasing that physique, she wants to look like what she sees as a real woman – curves and all. She continues to eschew the Hollywood stereotype of the figure-conscious rocket salad or carb-free diets, instead admitting happily that her favourite food is 'anything fried and carbs'. Driving the point home in an interview with *The Sun*, she added: 'Probably my favourite food is a potato – just a potato, because I like fries, boiled potatoes, mashed potatoes, baked potatoes.' As for people who say they are addicted to fitness and workouts, Jennifer gives them short shrift. 'I want to punch them in the face,' she told *Seventeen*.

What a breath of fresh air she is. 'It's hard for a

young woman because typically the roles you're offered are beautiful and bitchy, ugly and nice or pretty and stupid. I've been lucky to stay away from that,' she said of the gritty, authentic roles she has taken. Nor is she obsessive about getting her appearance right. For instance, she actively hates clothes shopping. Despite having ample funds and a host of advisers and stylists to help out, she finds the experience of clothes shopping 'torture'. When hair and make-up teams fuss over her, she admits to thinking, 'oh, no, I don't belong here'.

She has mixed feelings about fame itself. She is aware of an enormous pressure not to upset or disappoint her fans. 'It's scary, when you think . . . you're holding these characters that a lot of people are going to put a lot of weight into,' she told the *Washington Post*. She has come to terms with the fact that the publicity machine wants her to be 'likeable all the time' but knows that she cannot always manage to be so. She became so worried that she was an unlikeable interviewee that she consulted a magazine feature that offered interview tips. What she discovered there shocked her, as she explained later to *Interview* magazine. 'The article was basically about how to get someone not to hate you in twenty minutes. Every single thing they told you not to do, I was like, "I do that every day,"' she said.

She has to spend so much time away from home,

either filming on location or travelling on the publicity and award circuits, that she does miss home. 'It messes with your head,' she said. Indeed, at one point she even considered chucking in the job altogether. It was when people began to speak to her differently that she became unsettled. 'I couldn't stand that,' she declared. She noticed that where she was once essentially 'invisible' at parties, suddenly she was the centre of attention – and she felt spooked by it. She wondered whether she might be happier in a different part of the industry. As people suddenly began to treat her with such reverence, she realized why some famous actors ceased to behave normally: it was because the world had ceased to treat them as normal.

Lest the impression be given that Jennifer is yet another celebrity who relentlessly chases fame only to then complain about it, she is clear over how fortunate she is. While she hates shopping, she loves being able to own masses of designer gear, with Louis Vuitton, Forever 21 and Proenza Schouler among her favourites. She also loves how her needs are attended to so well on-set. 'Everybody's like "Oh, do you need water? Here's forty-five bottles!"' she told *Elle* magazine. She also enjoys being considered a sex symbol and believes, overall, that she is now in 'wonderland'.

Working with big names is also a thrill for her

– and she got to do just that in 2009 when she was chosen for *The Beaver*, which boasted cinematic royalty Jodie Foster and Mel Gibson in its cast. Foster also directed the drama. Jennifer said that the two ladies saw plenty of themselves in one another. 'We both walked away thinking the same thing: "I've never met anybody who reminds me of me more,"' she said in the book *Beyond District 12*. These were bold words for a rising actor to utter about a senior star, yet Jennifer has rarely lacked courage. 'We both think of this as a job, and don't understand why you suddenly have to become an asshole when you become successful at it,' she added. She said both actresses also shared an attitude towards direction. Jennifer's co-star Anton Yelchin said of the youngster that she 'finds strength in every moment', identifying a trait which has led to her being offered so many characters with painful pasts and presents.

The release of *The Beaver* was delayed for two years, by which time Jennifer had taken further steps upwards in stature. As well as filming the romantic drama *Like Crazy* and the dark thriller *Devil You Know*, she landed a part in the prequel for the juggernaut-like *X-Men* franchise. There, she would meet a young man who would change her life – but she nearly turned the opportunity down. When 20th Century Fox offered her a part in the film she spoke to her mother, and even after talking it over with Karen, Jennifer was not clear about what she wanted to do. She feared that the script would be bad, but when she finally got to read it she was pleasantly surprised.

Throw into the mix that two of her favourite actors – James McAvoy and Michael Fassbender – were already signed up, and there were factors drawing her to *X-Men*. Mindful that there would inevitably be sequels to come if she signed on, she took a long time to decide what to do. She feared that she could live to regret joining a sequel-heavy franchise. With the boost from the script fresh in her mind, she agreed to play Mystique. In this, her first action movie proper, Jennifer had to work hard on her body to prepare for the part. She ate a high-protein diet and worked out rigorously to get ready for when she appeared on-screen wearing nothing but a coat of blue paint. Each day for several months a team of make-up artists would spend several hours painting her blue. This required an enormous amount of trust and intimacy. 'Nothing's sacred anymore,' quipped Jennifer to *GQ*.

Among the cast was a handsome young English actor who caught her eye, as well as that of many of the film's subsequent teenage viewers. His name was Nicholas Hoult, who first came to public attention starring as an adorable lost twelve-year-old in the film *About a Boy*, which starred Hugh Grant. He was also well known to British television audiences, not least for his role in the raunchy E4 teen drama *Skins*. Rumours quickly emerged that he and Jennifer began dating during the filming of *X-Men*. The first sign that those rumours were correct came early in 2011, when they arrived at an industry bash together. Hoult was coy when probed for details by *The Guardian*. 'OK, well, you know, erm, Jen's great and we had lots of fun doing the film, and she's a very talented actress and . . . I'm just stepping around the question, basically!' he told the interviewer. Speaking about their love more recently, Jennifer told *Elle*: 'He's my favourite person to be around and he makes me laugh harder than anybody.' We will return to their complicated relationship in more depth in Part Two.

Cinematically, perhaps her most exciting part prior to *The Hunger Games* came in the romantic comedy-drama *Silver Linings Playbook*. For this part, she would play alongside the legendary Robert De Niro and man of the moment Bradley Cooper. Jennifer's character Tiffany befriends Cooper's, who is a teacher suffering with bipolar disorder, trying to rebuild his life. The characters' bond is touching, as is the film itself, which gently examines the human condition. Both stars are utterly compelling, as most of the critics agreed. The *Playlist* said that Jennifer and Cooper 'both arguably give career best, awards-worthy performances', and the *Hollywood Reporter* said they were 'a delight to watch'. *Time* magazine singled her out, saying: 'Just twenty-one when the movie was shot, Lawrence is that rare young actress who plays, who is, grown-up.' Even the *New Yorker*, which published an essentially negative review, was upbeat about Jennifer, conceding amid its general gloom that: 'Things improve a bit when the tough, direct Jennifer Lawrence shows up.'

It is hard to describe Jennifer's rise at this point as anything short of meteoric. Speaking to *The Sun*, she gave a no-nonsense assessment of the implications of that. 'When you get a promotion at your job, you don't go, "God, that was too fast, can I stay in the mailroom?"' she said. 'You kind of take it thankfully. It was fast, but I'm grateful for it.' The next role she was offered was to become her biggest to date. She knew it would be so and, as with *X-Men*, she had an attack of nerves and indecisiveness when she tried to make up her mind as to whether to take it or not. What ultimately swung her decision was that she did not want to turn a project down through lack of courage. Ever the fearless tomboy, she bit the bullet and took it on.

Chapter Three

LIAM:

IT'S IN THE FAMILY

Sibling rivalries have spurred many a young man on to greater things. A little healthy competition can be a great motivation, after all. It is quite a force at the best of times – but when those siblings are a bunch of tall, strapping, testosterone-fuelled young Australian men, the contest can become fierce. The youngest sibling is often the one most determined in such scenarios. Having grown up as the smallest in the family, they want to prove their strength. It was just this sort of force which first propelled Liam Hemsworth into acting. 'I saw my brother doing it,' Liam told *Interview* magazine, 'and I thought I could do it better.' He decided there and then that acting was what he wanted to do. 'I was lucky that it's worked out,' he said.

Liam was born on 13 January 1990 in the city of

Melbourne. He joined an already four-strong family. It may seem strange to think of the towering, six-foot-three Liam as a little brother but that is what he is. He was the third of three boys: before him had come Luke and Chris. His father Craig is a social services counsellor, while his mother Leonie was an English teacher. With both parents tied up in demanding professions, the boys often entertained themselves. Liam found that his brothers used to play pranks on him. For instance, they would put a couple of jumpers on Liam and then chase him around the backyard, shooting air rifles at him. 'I feel like the worst brother in the world,' said Chris, confessing to the pranks in an interview with *Details* magazine. 'But [Liam] had a great time, okay?' The youngest Hemsworth is not quite so upbeat about these childhood experiences. 'I'd bend over to feed the guinea pigs and I'd get a pellet in the ass out of nowhere,' he said. 'It really hurt.'

They must have been memorable experiences for the little boy of the family. However, in a separate interview, our man has admitted he was far from angelic himself at times – and was even awarded a satanic family nickname. 'When I was a little kid I was a devil,' he admitted during an interview with The Actors Factory. 'My brothers called me 666. I was seriously crazy.' He then went on to come clean about some very aggressive brotherly scraps and games. 'Once I even tried to stab them with real knives,' he said. 'Thank goodness when I got to about ten I started to mellow.' With air rifles and guns in the mix of the family games, it is indeed a good job that Liam began to mellow. Yet his desire to better his brothers would not subside.

Despite these hair-raising experiences he had growing up and the fractious atmosphere that sparked them, Liam insists he has always been comfortable in the youngest sibling role. As he told *Men's Health* magazine, whatever 'pickle' he finds himself in, he has two wise elder brothers to call on for advice. 'They've probably lived through whatever my problem is,' he said. Indeed, with seven years between the births of Chris and Liam, the youngest of the family felt very much just that. 'I'm the youngest so I've always looked up to my brothers and I was always influenced by what they were doing,' Liam has said. 'Maybe I wouldn't have become an actor if my older brothers weren't actors, but now that I'm here, I really enjoy it and it's what I feel more comfortable doing.'

Liam was born under the star sign of Capricorn. Given his childhood status as the sometimes satanic, knife-toting baby of the family, it is interesting to reflect that three key traits associated with the star sign are stability, calmness and maturity. Indeed, sceptics of astrology will note with a wry smile that several other traits associated with the sign – including shyness – are ones that are hard to square with a famous actor. More pertinently to Liam, Capricorns are renowned for their work ethic and determination to succeed no matter what. If there is truth in astrology it is to be found right here in Liam's story, in which both those traits continue to resonate strongly.

As with Jennifer Lawrence, nature and wildlife loom large in Liam's early years. Growing up, he experienced several different types of neighbourhoods. Prior to his birth, the family had lived in a secluded Aboriginal district of Bulman, deep in Australia's fabled outback. As Chris explained, 'My earliest memories were on the cattle stations up in the outback, and probably my most vivid memories were up there with crocodiles and buffalo.' He explained that the Hemsworth clan were in quite a minority. 'We were isolated, one of two white families,' he told the Australian edition of *GQ* magazine. 'We saw a lot of corroborees and tribal dancing. I have a wider understanding for the Aboriginal situation because of my time there. It's an insight into that world that most people don't get.' Then, he added, 'we moved to Melbourne and Liam came along.' Suddenly, their previously rural existence was replaced by a more metropolitan experience. Although they were on the suburbs of Melbourne rather than in the heart of the city, the change of surroundings for the family was still stark. The three boys rode the Melbourne trams and took advantage of the city's plentiful sporting venues.

There would be a fresh upheaval when Liam turned thirteen. With their youngest's primary school days behind him, his parents decided this was the right time to move to Philip Island. The island is located about 140 kilometres south-south-east of Melbourne. Having lived in the rural isolation of Bulman and then the brighter lights of suburban Melbourne, the family now resided on a tranquil and beautiful island of just thirty-nine square miles. With a population of around 7,000, it had an intimate feel. The house was remote: it was a fifteen-minute drive to buy milk and much further for anything more exciting than that. Liam could not see any other houses from the family home, which lay in a setting that could feel either blissful or unsettling, depending on the mood of the moment.

Liam joined a new high school and it was there that he met Laura Griffin, who would play a significant role in his life. She remembers that, far from being the nervous outsider, Liam quickly became the star turn at high school. His good looks, charisma and humour made for a dazzling combination. 'He was the new boy at school and all the girls liked him,' Griffin told *Woman's Day*. 'He was popular, a bit of a joker and made me laugh.' He also made for an imposing character, both physically and personality-wise. Like a golden boy from a high school movie, he made quite the impact. Liam was, then, not lacking for friends, but it was Griffin with whom he grew particularly close. Their bond became strong and developed into a multi-pronged relationship. They were like friends, lovers and siblings. These were idyllic times for them both. 'We became inseparable,' she said. 'He tried to teach me to surf, we watched movies, and went shopping. Liam became more than a boyfriend; he was my best friend.'

As is the case with many high-school golden boys, surfing has long been a passion for Liam. 'I've always loved surfing,' he said. 'When I was at school that was pretty much all that mattered in my life.' His hero is not an actor but American surf champion Kelly Slater, who has been crowned ASP World Champion a record eleven times, including five consecutive titles between 1994 and 1998. Liam loved other sports, too. He has said that, were he not an actor, his dream job would be as a basketball star in the NBA. At high school he also studied cookery. This has turned him into quite the chef. 'I'll do anything Italian, like spaghetti or pizzas,' he said. A surf, a hunk, a wit and a cook – Liam was already the sort of young man to win the hearts of girls long before he even took a step into the acting world, which would quickly make him a pin-up for millions.

His first part came in the Australian television series *McLeod's Daughters*. Launched in 2001 when Liam was just eleven, it follows the fortunes and struggles of half-sisters Claire and Tess McLeod on their cattle farm in the South Australian outback. Six years into its run, Liam took a small part in the series, portraying a teenager called Damon. It was a part that required him to only miss one week of classes, yet by the time he returned to school, the experience had turned the teenager's head. He found acting far more fun than lessons. 'When I came back, I just didn't want to be there anymore. My head wasn't in the same place and I knew I had to get out.' He also took a brief part in the popular Australian soap opera *Home and Away* in 2007. It was such a small part that the character was not given a name, but for Liam it was a big entry on his CV. Young actors love to have such notches on their record.

He was ready to move into acting full-time, yet that was easier said than done. Meanwhile, he took whatever jobs he could. 'I must have done every job you could do on the island,' he told *Vanity Fair*'s

Krista Smith. These included tasks as assistants to local labourers, plumbers and electricians, as an assistant at a bakery, at a bowling alley and at a nature park. He was also an usher at the island's yearly Penguin Parade ceremony. 'I feel thankful I got to do jobs like that,' he said. 'I feel lucky to have come from a hard working-class family, and to know what that sort of life is like.' He also took a slightly longer job laying floors for a construction company. The best he could say about this tough role was that it gave him some much-needed perspective for the years to come. 'I was laying floors for six months,' he told Melbourne's *Herald Sun*. He found the memory slightly chilling, but useful. 'It makes me really appreciate what I have got at the moment.'

One way he loved to relax after work was with a movie. Two of Liam's favourite films are *The Departed* and *Superbad*. The former film was released in 2006 when Liam was sixteen. It is a crime thriller set in Boston, directed by the legendary Martin Scorsese and starring Leonardo DiCaprio, Matt Damon, Jack Nicholson and Mark Wahlberg. *Superbad* was released the following year and is quite a different proposition. Starring the cute, nerdy Michael Cera and the hilarious Jonah Hill, it is a high-school comedy in which the two male leads attempt to get drunk and laid, with hilarious results. Yet it was watching these two very different films that helped fuel Liam's dreams.

His eyes remained on the prize of a career as a Hollywood actor. However, his first breakthrough came on the long-running Australian soap opera *Neighbours*. Set on Ramsay Street in Erinsborough, the soap was launched in 1985. It quickly became a hit in both Australia and Britain, where it was a lunchtime favourite before huge public pressure convinced the BBC to add a teatime repeat so schoolchildren and those with daytime jobs could also get a daily fix of their beloved Aussie drama. It became a hit in other countries, too, ultimately being shown in over fifty nations around the globe. It has launched the wider careers of now internationally famous stars including Kylie Minogue, Jason Donovan, Guy Pearce and Natalie Imbruglia. Liam's part in the show was a challenging one: he would play a paraplegic called Josh Taylor. Josh, who had become injured in a surfing accident, would become romantically involved with one of the series' key characters Bridget Parker, who was played by Eloise Mignon. Parker, too, was physically challenged, having been left paralysed down one side of her body in a car crash.

The couple's relationship would be an inspiring and emotional thread within the series – yet for both actors it took a lot of work to be able to portray such challenging roles. 'I just turned up on set, sat in a wheelchair,' he remembered. However, after the scene was filmed a producer announced that the entire thing would need to be re-shot. 'Your leg was moving,' he explained to Liam. His character met Bridget during physiotherapy sessions at a swimming pool. They had an on-off relationship which kept viewers glued to their sets. In time, Bridget broke off the relationship after deciding she wanted to return to her ex-boyfriend. Josh left Erinsborough, and the series, heartbroken. Yet, during his twenty-five episodes on-screen, he had made an impact on viewers and on the television industry. Fans were both gripped by the story and also educated by it; Liam and his co-star managed to break down many misconceptions about people who live with such conditions and challenges.

The world of soap operas was kind to the Hemsworths as they grew up. He had seen his brothers both appear in Australian dramas. Liam had followed Chris's footsteps into *Home and Away*, while Luke had portrayed John Carter in *Neighbours*. While Liam presented his wish to better his elder siblings in humorous terms, it was only natural for him to actually be very serious about outclassing them. In time, he would. First, he had to negotiate the hard work of moving up the ladder. To that end he accepted a role in a television series called *The Elephant Princess*. His role was as Marcus, a guitar-playing boyfriend of a girl who discovers she is the princess of a mystical Indian kingdom. Experiencing a variety of roles, he followed this children's television part with one in a much more adult affair: the drama series *Satisfaction*. Created by writer/producer Roger Simpson with producer Andy Walker and executive producer Kim Vecera, the series centres around the lives of women who work in '232', a high-class brothel. 'I played a sixteen-year-old who hires a prostitute,' he explained. 'I was butt-naked in front of fifty people, which is totally comfortable.' His sarcasm is finely tuned. *Neighbours* must have seemed a million miles away as he played such a role – even in its raciest moments, Ramsay Street would never feature such scandalous storylines.

Yet the series received plentiful praise from the *West Australian*: 'the characters are fleshed out, the drama is feasible and the script is sophisticated enough to sidestep the obvious clichés of the sex industry. While the setting and characters are glamorous and gorgeous, there are no *Pretty Woman*-style illusions about the job . . .' *TV Tonight* was slightly more measured, saying: 'for all its empathy *Satisfaction* is like dipping your toes into a warm bath and sipping on the best champagne. It skews consciously toward the high end of prostitution to ample success. But like their wealthy clients, you'll need to be a high-class customer of Foxtel to slip off your shoes first, an irony some programmers may have missed.' Since he found mega-fame through *The Hunger Games*, photographs of Liam in his *Satisfaction* role have become popular online items. Females – and some males – who fancy him were thrilled to learn he had such a raunchy entry on his profile.

Long before which, in 2008, Liam finally got the chance to do what he'd dreamed of for so long – to appear in a movie. He was approached by the makers of a new, British-made psychological horror thriller called *Triangle*. The film, written and directed by Christopher Smith, would co-star his fellow Australian actresses Melissa George and Rachael Carpani. Though it was a low-budget, cult-like ninety-nine-minute affair, here was a chance for him to excel. He took the role of Victor, one of a group of twenty-something passengers who get stranded on a deserted ship after their yacht venture goes wrong. As scarier and stranger things happen on the ship, the action becomes more terrifying and tense.

In the making of the movie, Liam learned things he had scarcely touched on during his television parts. He has admitted that he sometimes needs up to 'fifty' takes to get a scene right. Perhaps the longest sequence of takes for a scene he had ever been involved in came during *Triangle*, in which he had to strangle co-star Melissa George. 'It was a really hard scene to do because, obviously, you want it to look real but at the same time I don't really want to injure her,' he told the movie website Collider. 'So I had to come up to her and kind of slam her in the throat and then choke her. God, we did a lot, a lot of takes and it just got to the point where we both were like, "You've got it. We can't..." She was exhausted. It was really tough not to be hurting her in every take. I can't remember how many takes we did, but we did a lot.'

Although it was George's performance, rather than those of her co-stars, that garnered the most attention among the critics, that could not mask the fact that Liam's debut film had attracted fine notices from the reviewing community. *The Guardian* gave it three out of five stars, describing it as 'a rather smart, interestingly constructed scary movie', while *Time Out* praised its 'moving emotional reality'. The film moved Liam further onto the map. While the short-sleeved tops his character wore on-set attracted the attention of several female viewers, Liam's part in the film also served notice to Hollywood that there was a new potential hunk on the block. However, the film's commercial performance was modest.

His next role was in a science fiction disaster film called *Knowing*, which starred Hollywood legend Nicholas Cage. Born in 1964, Cage has appeared in over seventy films including *Leaving Las Vegas*, *The Rock*, *Kick-Ass* and *Ghost Rider*. In this film, Liam would play an MIT student. The film was shot in familiar territory for Liam: at Melbourne's Docklands Studios. It was a brief part, the bulk of which involves his character answering a question about the sun, which is posed by the teacher, played by Nicholas Cage. Cage throws a ball to Liam in asking the question, and Liam returns it as his own answer is completed.

For this film, the critics were harsh in some quarters. The *San Francisco Chronicle* called it 'a surprisingly messy effort'; the *Washington Post* deemed it 'predictable'; and the *Los Angeles Times* said some aspects of the film were 'cringe-inducing'. Yet Roger Ebert, film critic of the *Chicago Sun-Times*, felt it was 'a splendid thriller and surprisingly thought-provoking', while *The Guardian* deemed the film's conclusion to reach a 'spectacular and thoroughly unexpected finish'. Liam was able to shrug off the verdicts, as he knew, in reality, that his part was not big enough to have influenced them.

Liam was thrilled to be able to work with Egyptian-born director Alex Proyas. This more than made up for the small part he got in the film itself. 'I think I had two or three lines,' he later told Moviefone. 'That was really cool because I got to meet Alex Proyas and work with him for two days, but it was more the fact that the two days I was there, the camera was on Nicolas Cage most of the time and I could just sit there and watch him, which was really, really cool.' He learned a great deal from his studying: 'He's just so professional in what he does,' Liam continued. 'You know, he won't really talk to anyone between takes; he'll talk to the director, but he keeps very much to himself. He's just amazing; you can tell when he's looking at you that he's got so much going on in his head. There's so much going on in his eyes.' Liam perhaps learned more just by being a bystander than he did from his small part. He proved that he, like all who thrive in their paths, was open to learn.

In the wake of *Knowing*, it was time for Liam to finally take the step he had dreamed of for so long: he was moving to Hollywood. 'I think when I started acting, the whole time I was working towards one day coming to America,' he later explained to the Moviefone website. 'Hollywood, in particular, is seen to be the centre of this industry, and I was just waiting for the right time to come.' Although this was the move he had been hoping to make for some time, Liam did not make it lightly, nor without consideration of its stature. 'Going to the States was a huge step,' he says. 'I was always working towards one day going to Los Angeles, because it's where the biggest movies are made and where the biggest directors work, but it's an enormous decision.'

Liam stepped off the fourteen-hour Qantas flight Hollywood-bound. He had a three-month visa, which meant that if he did not find work in just ninety days he would be straight back to Australia. Time was against him and there were plenty of people who had faced just the same challenge and failed miserably. He actually felt he had tasted the bitterness of such failure ahead of two previous, aborted trips to Los Angeles. First, he was offered a part in Sylvester Stallone's film *The Expendables*. He was thrilled to land such a part and could not wait to get to work on the film, in which he was set to star alongside the likes of Bruce Willis, Micky Rourke and Jet Li. His agent phoned him one day to tell him that he had the part and that Stallone would be phoning him to discuss it. As an excited Liam told a friend: 'Rocky's gonna give me a call – no big deal!' The star did indeed phone Liam, who found it surreal to speak to a man who had been the iconic lead in several of his favourite films. He vowed to give his all on this project.

Imagine his frustration then, when he was

told that, actually, he was the expendable. Due to a major overhaul of the script, Liam was axed from the film, much to his disappointment and embarrassment. He took the news badly, saying it was 'a big kick in the guts'. 'My bags were packed,' he told *Details* magazine. 'I've celebrated with my friends. Then we got told the script got rewritten and it's not happening. I was devastated. Like, what the f***? I told everyone I'm leaving. I look like an idiot.' Both he and Chris had auditioned for a part in the Marvel epic movie *Thor*. Initially, Chris was eliminated from the process, while Liam remained in it. 'I was out of the mix and he was in the mix,' said Chris.

But Liam would soon be hit by further disappointment. The two brothers had worked together on their audition preparations for *Thor*; trying to second-guess what director Kenneth Branagh would be after. They put aside their usual competitiveness to create 'a bit of a team effort', *Prestige Hong Kong* magazine reported. Liam recalled how, as he became a finalist for a part, he wore flowing golden tresses for subsequent screen tests. 'It's a hard thing to pull off a blond wig, I won't lie', he told *Details*. However, at the last moment he was told that he was not going to get the part – instead it would go to his brother Chris. Like a biblical story, the younger brother had initially shone and then, just as he was to receive the metaphorical crown, the previously abandoned elder brother usurped him. Chris did not let the moment pass without a bit of brotherly banter. He told Liam that he would get him a *Thor* action figure and a ticket to see the eventual movie. Liam has joked that when he learned it was Chris taking the part he punched his older brother in the head. 'No, I'm happier for him to get it than someone else,' he said, more seriously. 'My brother's playing Thor! That's so cool.'

Still, he was excited to finally arrive in America. As well as taking to the charms of Los Angeles and the West Coast, he also travelled to the East Coast and its most famous point, New York City. He adored it there, saying, 'I love New York. It just reminds me of so many movies . . . I look up at buildings, and feel like Godzilla should be climbing up them or something. I tried to get out and see it a bit. I went out to a sushi place and they served me sushi on an oar!' How different the cramped, noisy city must have seemed to the man who grew up on a quiet Australian island. Then it was back to Los Angeles to continue his quest for his big break, with Chris sharing the challenge.

In the wake of two big disappointments, as he settled in Hollywood with his three-month visa heaping more pressure on him, Liam was fairly realistic about what was ahead. He recalls a growing tension as the calendar ticked down to his exit day. 'There was a moment,' he told *Details*, 'I was sitting at our manager's house with Chris. He booked *Red Dawn* and *Thor* in the same week. We were celebrating for him. But then it was like, "Yeah, I'm probably going to have to go home in a week." But I didn't want to! I love this town.' Within a matter of days, Liam would get the big breakthrough he had been dreaming of, too.

Chapter Four

LIAM:
HEARTTHROB STATUS

It proved to be an epic and life-changing seven days for the Hemsworth brothers: to add to Chris's double-helping of leading roles, Liam was called by Disney to be told he had landed the lead part of Will Blakelee in their forthcoming romantic blockbuster, *The Last Song*. 'It was a really, really happy week for us,' said Liam. As Chris has separately explained, the brothers sometimes have to pinch themselves to believe how well they are doing. 'We're always kind of asking each other, "How did we get in this position?"' he told Movieline. 'To be involved in any of this stuff is kind of a trip for us.' Liam's film, *The Last Song*, is a coming-of-age flick. Its star is the Disney graduate Miley Cyrus, who plays Ronnie. Following her parents' divorce, she is sent to live with her father in a secluded costal region.

Her relationship with her father is complex and it is only when Will Blakelee, played by Liam, appears on the scene that her true feelings are unravelled.

The happy week in which he landed that part was followed by a breathless month. With a couple of shirtless scenes in the movie script, Liam knew he had to be in as fine physical shape as possible for the role, so he started training immediately. 'I've always been pretty energetic, I grew up surfing and I do a lot of boxing and kickboxing and stuff so I was already pretty fit,' he said. However, in the lead-up to the filming of *The Last Song* he worked with a personal trainer six days a week. He was keen to add that this was a 'character decision', rather than vanity on his own part. 'He's a star volleyball player and he's athletic. I'm not going to have a six-pack for a film unless I have to. I'm going to stay true to the role.' Suitably, given Liam's mention of a six-pack, the famously ripped Taylor Lautner was among those previously considered for the role of Blakelee.

Liam also took classes in volleyball. Despite his varied sporting efforts, this was new territory for him. At the first day of practice, he felt 'honestly really scared' about the prospect of the volleyball scenes in the film, he told Collider, because he recognized 'it takes a lot of skills to play that game and I didn't have them at all'. He told the crew that they should consider hiring a double for the scenes, though he conceded: 'It's hard to find someone as big as me.' He also had to obtain a scuba certification to shoot some scenes and attended workshops on stained glass window making for others. However, at nineteen years of age, he suffered from plenty of nerves, too. 'It's a big deal,' he said. 'I was really scared. The biggest thing in my mind was not succeeding. That would have been embarrassing.'

He was unaware of the book *The Last Song*, but was familiar with other stories by author Nicholas Sparks. 'I'd seen *The Notebook* before and thought that was a really great story,' he said to Moviefone. On reading the script for *The Last Song*, he felt here was another great plot. 'I think Nicholas Sparks … he's got the power to affect people in some way or another. His stories incorporate so many different emotions, and have really good messages about family and love and friendship.' This, said Liam, was the key to their success. 'I felt the same way about this story; it's about a girl growing up and getting to know her father, and falling in love and dealing with responsibilities that come with that. And dealing with death, also.'

Liam would co-star with the singer Miley Cyrus. Alhough he had heard of her, he was unaware of her international fame. This, Liam explained in *Beyond District 12*, was a good thing, as it meant that when they first met on set he was meeting 'a girl', rather than a 'star'. Meeting her for the first time was, he recalled, 'great'. He added: 'she was so kind and so easy and really nice. Her music is awesome. She's incredibly talented.' His overall feeling having met her was 'pleasant surprise', particularly at her work rate. 'I don't know how she does what she does,' he said. 'Her work ethic is incredible.'

Miley's overall story is, indeed, bordering on the incredible. Born on 23 November 1992, she is the daughter of country music singer Billy Ray Cyrus and his wife, Tish. Her birth name was actually Destiny Hope but she smiled so much as a baby that her parents began to nickname her 'Smiley'. In time, this was shortened to 'Miley'. The family were based in Nashville, Tennessee for the formative years of her life, where she grew up alongside two siblings and three half-siblings. When she was eight, the family moved to Canada as her father had a television engagement there. By this stage, she had caught the performance bug and wanted to try her hand at acting.

Soon, she was making a cameo appearance in her father's series, *Doc*. She then got a small role in *Big Fish*, a Tim Burton movie. Next came the life-changing step: in 2004 she auditioned for a Disney television series called *Hannah Montana*. Her initial plan was not to try for the lead part but rather to apply for the back-up role of Hannah's best friend. Yet when the programme-makers saw her audition tape, they quickly earmarked her in their minds for the starring part. They asked her to audition directly for it and she impressed them so much they gave her the role. She had beaten 1,000 other shortlisted hopefuls, which was good going.

The Cyrus family moved to Los Angeles so that Miley could work on the series. Her father got a part on the show, too, as, appropriately enough, her father and manager. Quickly, her fame and reach were moving far beyond the boundaries of the Disney series. In 2006, she released a soundtrack album and in 2007 she put out a follow-up and embarked on a major tour. The following two years were even better: she reportedly earned $18.2 million in 2007 and her 3-D concert film netted $31.3 million in its opening weekend in February 2008. Having stepped out of the Disney fold, she was keen to rebrand herself with a more adult image. A raunchy photo shoot for *Vanity Fair*, taken by star snapper Annie Leibovitz, soon got that project rolling. A further album, an autobiography called *Miles To Go* and a *Hannah Montana* movie all helped her stature soar further. At which point her path crossed with that of Liam's.

The pair developed an instant rapport and chemistry. This is crucial, but not inevitable.

Jennifer, Liam and Josh

'For some people it can be an effort to find that chemistry, but we worked really well together,' Liam told *Dolly* magazine. 'It's a funny thing; I have known people who hate each other in real life but have amazing chemistry on screen. We don't hate each other in life. We get along really well so it just worked on screen – and we get along really well together in real life too.' However, in one important sense Liam felt that his real life and the life of his character, Will, were poles apart: 'I'm nothing like my character in the film, not at all, to be honest,' he told *Teen Vogue* magazine. For instance, Will's persistence when given the brush-off by Ronnie was in some contrast to Liam's way of operating with the opposite sex. 'If I was to get turned down by a girl, I'd just give up and say "Oh well,"' he explained. He said he lacks the 'motivation' to keep trying for a girl once she has turned him down. 'I would find that humiliating,' he added. As an acting pro, he had no problem portraying someone whom he felt differed from him. In fact, the biggest challenge was dealing with the fraught, emotional scenes. 'For me that's the hardest – bringing up that emotion. It's really hard to talk about anything very personal and emotional to a girl. I think that was the thing about Will and Ronnie and why they have a deep relationship; he realized that he could tell this girl anything at all.'

There were more physical challenges, too. For his first scene, he had to strip to his waist, exposing his newly honed chest. Then, he had a scene in which, unknown to him, he would kiss his co-star. 'It's funny,' he told Moviefone, 'because I didn't actually know there was going to be a kiss in that scene; it wasn't in the script.' The script had merely stated that he and Cyrus were running through water, 'having fun and splashing', he said. Then, as they filmed it, director Julie Anne Robinson shouted to them: 'Kiss!' It took him by surprise, but being a pro he followed her direction. 'And we kissed,' he said. 'It was kind of a good way to do it, because neither of us had time to get nervous about having a first kiss in front of a hundred people. It was good, we just got right into it, and then you've got the first kiss out of the way and you're fine!' He also ended up singing on camera – again to his surprise. 'That wasn't even in the script,' he said to *Dolly*. 'I just started singing along and then they said…"but that was so funny". I was laughing the whole way through that scene because I was like, "this is going to ruin my career!"' The reaction of Cyrus to his vocal efforts is unknown officially.

He called director Julie Anne Robinson 'amazing' and 'such a kind person'. He told *Dolly*: 'She always makes you feel really comfortable in a scene. It's just calm on set, which is great. You can relax and do your thing and she's very easygoing. She collaborates and often asked me: "What do you want to do in this scene and what do you feel about this scene?" It's great to be able to talk to a director like that and share ideas.' Yet he had found the experience exhausting. This was his first taste of film-making and here he was as the lead. He will always remember the first day filming, when he walked to the on-beach set and found one end of it with a fence blocking out the crowd of 'screaming kids' who had shown up to watch. 'I'd never seen that before,' he said. 'It was quite amazing.' Such scenes would become more familiar to him in the years ahead as he grew closer to Cyrus and as his own fame rocketed.

The film itself is a fine piece of heart-warming cinema. Liam's quietly brooding presence through much of it is central to its charm, even if Cyrus is the true star. The way his character sets about melting the heart of Cyrus's sultry lead, after he – quite literally – bumps into her for the first time, is bordering upon the masterful. She fears a 'stupid summer romance' with a 'stupid summer boy', and Liam's character must work hard to convince her it, and he, can be so much more than that. In doing so, he plays the quiet hero role more than competently. Among the challenging scenes is one, late in the film, when he gets involved in a fight with a bar-wielding thug at a wedding. All is well that ends well, though: the film closes with the two lovers kissing on the beach.

The reviewing community was far from kind to *The Last Song* as they penned their write-ups. Much of the criticism focused on Cyrus rather than Liam, and a fair amount of that seemed to be motivated more out of an inherent distaste for the very casting of the squeaky-clean Cyrus rather than any genuine problem with her performance. The storyline itself was also attacked and again this was no reflection on Liam's part. Nevertheless, the reviews would have stung. Rob Nelson of *Variety* magazine wrote that, 'Cyrus, alas, hasn't yet learned not to act with her eyebrows and overbite'. In the *Ottawa Citizen*, Jay Stone was only a little kinder, writing: 'Cyrus doesn't have a lot of range'. The *New York Times* said that Liam's co-star 'play-act[s] rather than exploring the motives and feelings of her character'.

Yet he would win awards for his role, including the gong for Teen Choice Awards 2010 male breakout star and, shared with Cyrus, the honour of Nickelodeon's 'fave kiss' of 2010. The outside world had not realized, at first, that the kisses Liam shared with Cyrus on-screen were continuing off-screen, too. He had recently broken up with long-term girlfriend Laura, while Cyrus too was said to be newly single. She had previously dated the pop star Nick Jonas, the young actor Tyler Posey, and the model Justin Gaston. 'I was actually going through a tough time,' she told the *Examiner*. 'Guys needed to be out of my life for a little while and I just wanted to focus on my work.' Indeed, so heartbroken was she that she arrived to shoot the film 'crying harder than I had ever cried in my life'. Thanks to Liam, she would leave 'with the biggest smile on my face'.

When she met Liam, Miley was immediately struck by his good manners. It was the most simple of gestures that won her attention. As she told *The Ellen DeGeneres Show*, 'I met him and he opened the door for me, and I was like, I have been in LA for three years and I don't think any guy has actually opened the door for me. It wasn't that he wanted the job. That's just who he is.' She found him, she said, 'super impressive'. As far as she was concerned, 'He's hot and he opened the door – excellent!' She loved this instance of what she called 'old-school chivalry'. Despite the instant attraction this gesture caused, it was a slow process for her to fall for him entirely. 'We started filming and at one point the chemistry was kind of awkward,' she said. 'I liked him a little bit, he liked me a little bit, but it was awkward. Then I was like, "Ok, just fake it."' She asked Liam to pretend he liked her. 'I don't have to pretend,' he replied. 'I really do like you.' Cyrus was pleased. She thought, 'Ok, you're going to be my boyfriend. Cool.' Liam, too, felt a speedy connection with her. 'From the first time we read, it was like I had known her before,' he is quoted as saying in the book *Beyond District 12*.

Cyrus was delighted by her latest catch. 'I got a hot boy!' she told E! Online. She purred that Liam was 'not bad to look at for the summer'. She also quipped that she was secretly behind the hiring of Liam for the part. 'I said to Nicholas Sparks, "I like animals, I like music, I like hot Australians,"' she said. 'It worked out fine, and I owe Nicholas, big time!' As for Liam, a key thing he admired in Cyrus was her frankness and honesty. 'I like to put things on the table,' he told *Seventeen*. 'I like when other people do that as well – you don't really get anywhere if you keep it all bottled up. You need to talk about it.'

However, when speaking more seriously she and Liam were both less than candid as to the nature and depth of their relationship. Cyrus told MTV: 'it sucks when your personal life becomes public. So I'm finding ways to make my personal and private life more of my life – which is one of the reasons I deleted my Twitter.' Speaking to *Seventeen*, she added: 'we've decided that any type of relationship that we have, we will always just keep it very DL. First and foremost, we are best friends, so that's what I tell people all the time.' Separately, Liam did, indeed, echo this policy, stating: 'we are great friends. We shot a film together for three months and we are both really proud of the work we did in that film and, yeah, we are great friends.' Physically, they were perhaps an unlikely partnership. Liam stands at a towering six foot three, while the famously short Cyrus is a mere five foot four. 'He's really tall,' Cyrus told *Teen Vogue*, rather stating the obvious.

These coy, carefully worded statements did nothing to dampen the fire of the celebrity media, however. Few stories get the show-business journalists more excited than the prospect of a celebrity coupling. They sharpened their metaphorical pens in the hope of landing an official, copper-bottomed story of the pair's rumoured romance. Duly, the pair eventually came clean about their love. For Liam, this amount of openness with the media was outside of his comfort zone. 'I get nervous talking about my private life,' he told ClevverTV, 'but it's hard to deny . . . so many photos.' He was soon stepping out of his comfort zone in speaking more and more openly about his feelings for Cyrus and about their lives together. Sometimes, he clothed his words with a light covering of humour, to lift the mood and displace his uneasiness in speaking about such a personal matter. 'There is this place in Nashville,' he told an interviewer for *Who* magazine, referring to the place of his girlfriend's birth, 'called Steak and Shake, which is pretty much the best food, ever.

That is our secret, sexy place to go. When I look over at her when she's biting into a steak sandwich and there is some steak sauce dripping down her chin, there is nothing sexier than that.'

When they visited Liam's family home on Philip Island, again the focus of their time together seemed to be around food. He introduced his girlfriend to a local eatery called Dr Food. There, she quickly developed a favourite dish. In fact, she became obsessed with it. The 'Dr Food meat pie with macaroni cheese' is, as Liam put it to the *Herald Sun*, 'like chicken pot pies but only with beef – they're pretty much the best thing ever'. Cyrus seemed to agree and made sure they made several returns to Dr Food during their visit to the island. Not that she was feeling homesick – in fact, she felt eerily at home on the island. When she first saw the area he lived in, she said: 'Oh my gosh, this looks like Nashville!' She explained later to Yahoo! Voices: 'there were, like, cows everywhere. I am, like, "How are you from the opposite side of the planet and your world looks just like mine?"' Liam begged to differ. Digging deeper than the unremarkable coincidence of cows existing in both areas, he insisted that Philip Island is 'a completely different world to where she's from'. Most importantly, the visit had been a success, not least because his parents 'loved' his new girlfriend.

Meanwhile, the couple were finding that despite

these stints of travel in close proximity, their bond was only stronger. 'I've never gotten along with someone so well,' beamed Cyrus to MSN. She explained that they had first moved in the direction of becoming an item after their first scene together, the one that included the famous 'kiss'. Even though the 'last thing [she] was expecting to do was fall in love', that is exactly what ended up happening. She found that she and Liam would balance each other out on-screen, each bringing the best out of the other. To her surprised pleasure, the same would happen off-screen, too: they really complimented one another. Completing the virtuous circle, their feelings for one another off-screen then boosted their on-screen chemistry. She felt dizzy over it all, telling herself, 'Girl, here is this amazing guy!' As they got to know each other better, she told *US Weekly*, Liam became her 'best friend in the whole wide world – I love him'. It is interesting that, like Laura, she spoke of Liam as being as much of a good friend as a partner.

Liam remained unsure of the wisdom of sharing too much of their lives with the public, developing techniques to remind himself of the importance of how things were going in private. 'The main thing is that we know how we feel,' he told *Beyond District 12*. 'We know what's going on. It can get complicated bringing the rest of the world into it.' He also developed a policy of dealing with the paparazzi, whose growing attention left the Aussie feeling 'frustrated'. He decided that the 'best thing to do' was to give them a smile and then get on with his day. 'If you do anything else you just end up looking stupid anyway. Whatever you do, you have to think about – so I definitely leave the house with pants on. Usually.'

His relationship with fame was a complex one from the start. Like many modern celebrities, it has at its heart a contradiction: he works tirelessly in a profession in which fame is an inherent feature, but then complains when his efforts result, inevitably, in attention. His relationship with Cyrus, which started some years before his own level of celebrity rocketed due to *The Hunger Games*, gave him a taste of what was in store for him in the future. While his status as the other half of Miley Cyrus gave him an instant boost of his own via proxy, he was also able to observe the utter craziness of his girlfriend's global fame from a short distance. For instance, when they attended the Oscars ceremony, he enjoyed the glitter of it all and the star-studded audience while Cyrus was singing on-stage. 'It was my first big event and it was really cool to be inside one of those things and see it all happen, to see all the actors and musicians walking around.'

That heady combination of his famous girlfriend,

of whom much more later, and his own fairly rapid rise within the film industry had taken him to the places he had dreamed of in earlier years. Liam, the little boy of the Hemsworth family, had risen to not only physical heights; he had also already proven himself against his elder brothers in the sphere of acting. What would happen next for him would dwarf these achievements.

Chapter Five

JOSH:
YOUTHFUL AMBITION

Joshua Ryan Hutcherson was born on 12 October 1992 and, almost from the start, he was in a hurry to define his own existence and decide on his path in life. By the time he was four years of age, he had settled on a plan: he told his parents that he wanted to become an actor who would star on television and in film. In one of his first ever interviews, as a tender-featured eleven-year-old kid, he told the *Cicncinati Enquirer* that his calling had actually begun even earlier than that: 'Since I was three years old, I wanted to entertain people. I liked to watch TV, and I always thought, "How cool it would be to be like them."'

In life, one sometimes meets people who are middle-aged and still unsure what career path they want to take in life. No activity has sufficiently caught their imagination nor filled them with enough passion to find a job that makes them tick. How remarkable that Josh had managed to do just that when he was little more than thirty-six months old. Yet where Josh was all hurried ambition, his parents were cautious and pragmatic. They wanted to support their firstborn in his dreams but also wanted to make sure he did not end crashing head first into disappointment or worse. Working their way around these conflicting feelings would become a feature of Hutcherson family life in the coming years.

The year of Josh's birth was a dramatic one. Riots broke out in Los Angeles after a video surfaced of police beating black man Rodney King, and Mike Tyson was convicted of rape. In a more positive development, President Bush and President Boris N. Yeltsin of Russia proclaimed a new era of 'friendship and partnership' as they declared the end of the Cold War. Top films to hit the big screen that year included *The Bodyguard*, *Aladdin*, *Basic Instinct* and *Batman Returns*. Musically, the grunge movement was peaking, with Nirvana hitting number one in the US charts.

Josh's parents, Chris and Michelle, were childhood sweethearts who first met at Grant County High School in Dry Ridge, Kentucky. Chris worked for the Environmental Protection

Agency in Clifton as a management analyst. Michelle found work as an emergency response trainer with Delta Airlines, though she would in due course surrender her own career path in order to support Josh in his. They were delighted when they had their first child together and it did not take the doting parents long to pick up on their son's theatrical leaning. 'Ever since he's been little, he's liked to perform for people,' said Chris. The proud father noticed that Josh was not merely an everyday attention-seeking kid, but one who had a natural ability to really deserve the spotlight. 'He has a personality that attracts people's attention,' he beamed.

One of the earliest photos of Josh in wide circulation features him sitting at the family kitchen table, with some homework books in front of him. However, Josh's attention is not with the books. Instead, he is pointing at his mother with a cheeky look on his face. She, in turn, is pointing back with a knowing smile. It is as if she both publicly disapproves but sneakily sanctions his cheeky manner. It is a touching image, and a revealing one, too: Michelle increasingly realized that she and Chris had someone special on their hands in their firstborn. Chris said he resolved to nurture and encourage his son. 'He does have talent,' he told the *Enquirer*, 'And it's part of a

Jennifer, Liam and Josh

parent's responsibility, if your child wants to do something, support him whenever you can.' As we shall see, Josh's memory of his parents' attitude to his ambitions is slightly at odds with those words.

Meanwhile, a younger brother, Connor, would join the family. Josh was excited, a little envious and rather fascinated to have a younger sibling. Unlike his future *Hunger Games* co-stars, then, Josh grew up as an eldest child. Typical characteristics of firstborns are an extended eagerness to please, and a pronounced likelihood to conform to rules. However, firstborns are likely to show responsibility or leadership in crisis situations. They can also be nurturing and caring but need to look out for attacks of self-criticism and envy, emotions that were first sparked the day they realized they were no longer the only child of the household, and watched as their parents' attention and affections were moved in part towards someone else. Josh is, in a fundamental sense, therefore a different personality to Jennifer and Liam, if you buy into birth-order theories. Nowadays he ranks Connor as the member of the family he is closest too, so any childhood resentments have evaporated.

As a child, Josh comforted himself in sadder moments with a pair of imaginary friends, who he called 'Hamo' and 'Damo'. He does not know why he gave them those names but he enjoyed their virtual friendship. He loosely viewed Hamo as the female of the pair and Damo as the male. He loved how when he was sent to his room for being naughty, his two buddies would be there for him. 'We'd sing Barney [the Friendly Dinosaur] songs together, as embarrassing as that is,' he said. One suspects many of his fans find this rather touching. He also developed another friend, of sorts, in the shape of a favourite comfort blanket, called 'yellow blankie', which he carried around with him everywhere. The peak era of yellow blankie was, he recalled, during his sixth and seventh years, yet it carried on after that – embarrassingly enough. One day, his parents sat him down and told him he was 'getting kind of old' for a comfort blanket. The item was in a gnarled and matted state. Eventually, boy and blanket parted ways – but not before Josh had reached ten years of age. What a rite of passage!

His unconventional friends had kept him company during many an otherwise boring childhood day, during which Josh's imagination would run riot. 'I was also obsessed with *Teenage Mutant Ninja Turtles* when I was younger,' he said. 'So obsessed that every time I'd walk over a drain, I'd bend over and say: "Hi, turtles!"' However, his real pop-culture obsession was the superhero Batman. 'I dressed like Batman, I had every single possible Batman toy on the planet,' he told TeenHollywood. 'My favourite toy of all time I think was this big giant bat cave that I had. I put Batman in there and little things would shoot out, he'd slide across the rope and that was so much fun.' As for Josh's own super-heroics, well, they did not always go to plan. He broke his elbow one day while playing around on some monkey bars. Impressively, though, he learned to swim that same summer, reportedly while still wearing a cast from the monkey-bars accident, which showed huge resilience on that occasion.

Meanwhile, his obsessive and imaginative mind also led to him having 'really bad' nightmares about the Wicked Witch of the West character from *The Wizard of Oz*. 'In my dream,' he explained, 'I would open my eyes and look out the window, and she would be there! I'd wake up scared to death!'

Some actors develop an interest in movie direction later in life. While some of the results have been hellishly embarrassing, should Josh ever take such a path there is a good chance that he could make something of a success of it, as he has always had the creative mind of the behind-the-camera crew. His imagination might have been more focused on him as a star, yet it is the depth of that imagining that suggests he could cross the divide from cast to crew one day. 'Every time I read anything, whether it be a book, a script or anything, I automatically imagine myself as the boy in the plot,' he told Hollywood Life.

Indeed, as a child, Josh possessed such a creative and confident mind that he felt some opportunities to perform were both stilted and dated. For instance, he found school plays nothing short of cringeworthy. 'I honestly dreaded doing school plays,' he told *DIY*. 'I hated it so much, not because I had stage fright, but because I thought the subjects were cheesy. They were like 1950s shoo-bop showaddy waddy and it made me mad.' He recalled with particular disgust an occasion when he was asked to sing 'horrible' 1950s songs at a grandparents' day at his elementary school. 'I was okay, thinking, fine I'll just go up there and mouth the words "watermelon" over and over again and pretend you're singing,' he continued. So he did so, feeling, he said, 'all angry and pissed off'. His grandmother had noticed exactly what he was doing as she sat in the audience. She confronted her eight-year-old grandson about it later, letting him know she knew exactly what he had been up to. He is unrepentant: 'I loved entertaining people and my family, but I never wanted to do it in a school play,' he said.

His first school was New Haven Elementary on US Highway 42. The establishment's ethos set him up well on the path he had chosen. For instance, the school curriculum lists five lifelong guidelines: 'Be Truthful, Be Trustworthy, Active Listening, No Put Downs, Personal Best.' It then fleshes its mission out, adding a wider list of life skills, from integrity to perseverance and sense of humour. These skills would serve Josh well in his show-business quest. As would another of them – 'patience'. He would have not just the vagaries of the industry to contend with, but the cautious nature of his parents, too. They were the first obstacle he had to negotiate; and he had to do that long before he could even go and face the endless obstacles of the industry itself.

Josh's recollections of the level of support his parents gave to his burgeoning ambitions contrast with those of his father. Josh says that his parents encouraged him to set aside his dream and instead take up sports. This was not for any cruel reason – they were just unsure of whether the ambition might be more of a passing fancy. Indeed, the sporting suggestion was not one plucked out of the ether, for Josh is a keen sports fan. 'My second passion is football, soccer and being a normal kid is what's great about what I do,' he told TeenHollywood. His favourite sports team is, reportedly, Cincinnati Bengals. He also loves music. Just before he submerged himself in the world of acting, Josh actually tried his luck in another entertainment sphere: that of rapping. 'It's a long story, but the short end is that when I was around nine, I think, I opened for the boy band O-Town,' he said. 'Well, not all by myself, but, with Rich Cronin (lead singer for LFO). I did, like, two rap songs with him on stage in front of a few thousand people. It was awesome, but I think I'll stick with acting!'

First, he *still* had to convince his parents, though. They were aware that the movie industry was a minefield of disappointment and darker forces. 'I had to beg and beg my parents since I was three or four years old,' he told the Miss O & Friends website. 'They heard all this negative stuff about Hollywood and being an actor.' He thinks the fact the family were based in Kentucky, rather than somewhere more show-business-related, worked against him, too. Michelle, for her part, recalls that Josh 'bugged' his parents. 'He wanted to do it. I have no clue why. We just thought, "He's a kid, he doesn't know what he wants."' However, in time, their son's relentless pressure paid off. 'And finally, he just pushed and pushed enough that I said I'd look into it,' said Michelle. 'And I did. And this is where it went, all of a sudden.' Josh remembers well how he finally won and the symbolism that marked it: 'Finally, they opened the Yellow Pages and we met an acting coach.'

The name of the acting coach was Bob Luke and he worked at the Heyman Talent Agency in

Jennifer, Liam and Josh

Oakley, California. Michelle took Josh to meet Luke in October 2001. Luke was impressed with what he saw in Josh. The boy's talent, drive and wholesome American looks made him an appealing prospect for the industry. He recommended a handful of Hollywood agents they could speak to and also told them to fly to Los Angeles as soon as possible and audition for television shows. Pilot season in Hollywood was just around the corner and Luke felt Josh had a chance of being snapped up at one of the try-outs. However, again his parents needed some convincing. 'I was so excited and begged and begged and begged,' recalled Josh.

Again, his unceasing pleas paid off – in January 2002 they headed for Hollywood to see what it could offer them. The journey to Tinseltown is one that is very well trodden. While some have managed to remain there and become household names, the route out of Hollywood is also a busy path. Here, the bitter disappointment forms a sharp contrast to the excited expectation of the route in. 'It's not all glamorous,' Josh later told Miss O & Friends. 'I learned that right away. I thought getting into acting would be a breeze, and nice and easy. I thought, "How hard could it be?"' When he and Michelle set off for Hollywood to find out, they left Chris at home. She had given up her job in order to support Josh in his dream, but the family did not want Chris to also surrender his job. 'Moving to LA would mean that Chris gives up his career and we don't want to do that,' Michelle told the *Cincinatti Enquirer*. 'Sometimes child actors don't have very long careers, and then we would have given up our home and Chris's career. We really like keeping our home as home, because that's where all our family is.'

Short careers are among the mildest of perils that threaten child stars, as so many of that breed have shown down the years. There are plenty of examples of child stars gone bad, few of them more chilling than Macaulay Culkin. Born in 1980, ten years later he became internationally famous for portraying Kevin McCallister in the movie *Home Alone* and then its sequel *Home Alone 2: Lost in New York*. His cute features and fine way in front of the camera made him a globally adored child. However, within four years he had grown so disillusioned with the industry that he retired at the tender age of fourteen. He had become friends with the pop star Michael Jackson and would in time be busted for various drug offences. His half-sister died of a drug overdose as Macaulay's life darkened further, and a source told the *National Enquirer* that the young man was 'hooked on drugs and it's killing him'. Increasingly shocking photographs of him have been published in newspapers across the planet. The once wholesome boy was now a wasted-looking adult, the shocking symbolism of his fading youth clear for all to understand.

Other child stars to fall from grace include Drew Barrymore, who won our hearts as cute Gertie in *E.T.*, but then entered a highly rebellious era which included smoking cigarettes before her teens, drug use in her very early teens and rehab at fourteen. She also attempted suicide. Then there is Jodie Sweetin, the star of *Full House*, who later admitted that she was struggling with an addiction to crystal meth. Similar meltdowns have occurred among pop stars that found fame particularly young. Britney Spears, who danced her way into the world's attention wearing a school uniform in a pop video, has admitted to taking drugs and stunned the world when she abruptly shaved all her hair off during an emotional meltdown. Yet a former manager says her drug use is even more serious than thought. He alleges that when she shaved her hair off, it was to conceal evidence of class-A drugs in her hair. Then there is Calkin's famous friend Michael Jackson, who became famous as a kid and whose own well-documented descent into craziness long preceded his premature death in 2009.

So the reader can perhaps understand the reticence of Chris and Michelle to simply allow Josh to dive head first into the acting trade. So many perils lie in wait there, particularly for children. First, Josh found work appearing in television commercials, as had Jennifer Lawrence. He showed up on-screen in advertisements for top companies including McDonald's, Kellogg's Mickey's Magic cereal, Ace Hardware and Kroger. These opportunities gave him much-needed experience on-camera, some entries on his acting CV and, of course, some money to help fund his continued presence in Los Angeles. His commercial work was not his ultimate goal but it was sensible of Josh to take it on, as it got his foot on the ladder.

The first acting part he got was in a Warner Bros. television comedy called *House Blend*. Josh was absolutely thrilled when he landed the part in the spring of 2002. The work kept coming: next up he appeared in the Animal Planet movie *Miracle Dogs*. Here, he played the part of Charlie, who was the son of a character played by Kate Jackson, the former star of *Charlie's Angels*. During the film he took a puppy round to patients at a hospital to cheer them up. 'It was all good, wholesome family fun. It makes you feel really good that you're doing something for somebody that they get to watch,' said Josh in a television interview to promote the movie. Sat nervously in a director's-style chair, he is wearing a yellow T-shirt and awkwardly grips the arms of the chair as he speaks.

Jennifer, Liam and Josh

Although he had surrendered rapping by this stage, he still had dreams to enter the world of comedy. 'I try and make people laugh,' he continued. 'I want to be a comedian, kind of. Like, Adam Sandler is a big idol.' Asked how he had got along with the cast and crew, he says 'they're really nice', adding that he had met 'some of the nicest people here'. Among the cast were the former star of *The Golden Girls* Rue McClanahan and Stacy Keach. His nerves subside when he is asked whether he hopes his friends at school will see the film. With a big, excitable grin, he says: 'Yes – big time! Then I'll be, like, popular!'

His animation at that point is sparked by the bullying he was encountering at school due to his involvement in the acting world. As he told TeenHollywood, when he started acting he faced 'a lot of crap' from his classmates. It was jealousy as much as anything but poor Josh was puzzled by their attitude. 'They were being really mean and I didn't understand because I just loved doing it and I didn't know what was wrong with it,' he said. 'It was hurtful to me, but I figured out after going through all of that, that you kind of have to let it go and just let them do that. Eventually if you don't let it bother you, they'll stop because that's what they like. They like seeing you kind of getting all upset about it.' Although, as we shall see, Josh has turned his experiences into a positive by campaigning on behalf of bullying victims, a question mark hangs over how at peace he is with his own childhood experiences. Speaking to MTV, for instance, he denied he was bullied at school. 'I was very fortunate and didn't personally encounter any bullies in school, however bullies exist in many ways in life,' he said. 'I think the best thing you can do is be secure in who you are and realize that the person who is bullying is the one you should feel sorry for their lack of knowledge. Bullies are just ignorant.'

The contradictions in his statements about his own experiences suggest an interesting psychology. Indeed, Josh himself had something of the therapist's curiosity about people from an early age. He believes that this dimension of his mind was a key factor in his decision to become an actor. 'Honestly, even as a little kid, at nine years old getting into acting, I think that's what drove me in the first place; that curiosity about people,' he told TeenHollywood. 'Everyone has so many different thoughts and ideas. Every person you walk by is just as complicated as you are. It's almost impossible to get your brain around the fact that there are so many different people in the world with so many different thoughts.'

In the video interview for *Miracle Dogs*, Josh's

nerves cannot cloud the fact that, even here, he is clearly a shining live wire, overflowing with charisma. The movie poster featured a beaming Josh holding puppies. He had so excelled as the adorable kid of *Miracle Dogs* that the industry was soon earmarking him for similar roles. Suddenly, Josh was being chased as much as he was chasing. But not everything was going his way in Tinseltown. Many of the auditions he attended were unsuccessful. He had a frustrating number of near misses, some of them for parts in what went on to become big movies. For instance, he tried out for *Home Alone 4*, the latest instalment of the franchise that had brought the world Macaulay Culkin. Josh would also be turned down for roles in *The Cat in the Hat* and *Bringing Down the House*. Unaware at this stage that he would, within years, become part of one of the biggest Hollywood movie franchises of all time, Josh took these rejections to heart. But around this time he dodged a rebuff of a different kind when he had his first kiss. He was eleven years of age. He has not elaborated on the experience but it came during a period in which he was awakened to romance. For instance, he is secretly very fond of the 2003 film *How to Lose a Guy in 10 Days*. Directed by Donald Petrie, it stars Kate Hudson and Matthew McConaughey.

Meanwhile, the next part he successfully won

was Chris Morse in the TNT movie *Wilder Days*. Here, things took a huge step up as far as Josh and his family were concerned. For a start, a poster promoting the film had Josh plastered upon it, alongside Tim Daly and Peter Falk. Michelle will never forget the day she first saw it in its full-sized glory on one of Hollywood's most famous streets, and neither will her son. 'I honestly started crying when I saw the billboard,' she told the *Enquirer*. 'You never imagine that one day your eleven-year-old son would be on a billboard on Sunset Boulevard in the middle of Hollywood. Josh just started screaming when he saw it!' It did not seem long ago that they had first arrived in the city, full of hopes and fears for the future. Here was physical proof they had made it.

Josh really enjoyed playing the part of Morse, who accompanies his sick grandfather on a trip so the old man can verify the magnificent stories of his life. David Mickey Evans's picturesque road trip turns into quite the diverting yarn. When his grandfather becomes ill, Josh's character got the chance to drive the golf caddy. 'He was so tired, and he pulled over at a rest stop,' Josh recalled. 'I was looking around, and heard scary noises, so I got in the car and just drove away, and tried to find a hotel. Then I hit a deer. And I get out and try to bring it back to life with jumper cables, because that was one of his stories. I sat in the driver's seat, while the stunt coordinator was low down in the car, and he pressed the gas and brakes. I just steered the wheel.'

His co-star Daly was mightily impressed with Josh, having worked with him on the film. 'He's an exceptional kid. He's a really good actor, and he's very smart and very confident in himself,' Daly told the *Enquirer*. His acting coach at the time, Selena Smith, was also aware of Josh's self-assurance. 'Some kids are just special. Josh is special. He's a natural,' she said. Josh was also attracting plaudits for the fact he had made such progress without ever setting foot on-stage at Cincinnati's School for Creative and Performing Arts, Playhouse in the Park or Ensemble Theatre. 'This is truly a one-in-a-million kind of thing . . . an extraordinary situation,' Terrell Finney, head of opera, music theatre, dance and arts administration at the University of Cincinnati's College-Conservatory of Music, told the *Enquirer*. 'The fact that he's had none of that (local) experience is amazing. This just simply doesn't happen,' added Finney. Recalling later in TeenHollywood how it had all come together, Josh said: 'I was so excited.'

Meanwhile, Michelle and Chris concentrated on keeping their excited son grounded. Michelle said that a lot of people who had met Josh would approach her to say, 'He's so professional, yet he's still a kid.' She was delighted to hear this, as she and Chris had wanted exactly that for him from the moment they first gave in to his pleas. 'We work hard to keep his life as normal as it can be,' she told the *Cincinnati Enquirer*. She explained that he was not allowed to 'just go out and buy things'. Instead, any big treats he wanted would be purchased over a period of months in instalments. 'His three big purchases – a dirt bike, a laptop and a gas-powered motor scooter – have been spread out over eighteen months,' she said. Indeed, he had been the last kid in his neighbourhood to get his hands on a motorized scooter. 'We didn't let him (at first)', said Michelle proudly. Instead, they set him to work doing household chores to earn the right to the scooter.

In a nutshell, she said, Josh had remained so grounded and young because his family let him be a kid. This was the perfect outcome for them – they did not want Josh becoming one of those precociously mature child stars that miss their childhood and speak with the weariness of middle age while still in their teens.

Chapter Six

JOSH:
THE HOLLYWOOD YEARS

Chris and Michelle's cautious, careful parenting frustrated Josh at times. But they had instilled in him a strength of character that only aided his career. While the Hutchersons tried to keep their expectations in check, things looked very good for the youngest son. Josh landed a part in an indie film. *American Splendor* is a refreshing blend of fiction and reality, which illuminates the life of comic book hero everyman Harvey Pekar, played by Paul Giamatti. The film won a significant award: the Grand Jury Prize at the 2003 Sundance Festival. It went on to attract further gongs from the Writers Guild of America and at the 2003 Cannes Film Festival.

In 2004, Josh continued to work away and landed a part voicing a character called Markl in the animation *Howl's Moving Castle*. This led to a similar role in a much larger film: the instant Christmas classic *The Polar Express*. Playing the child character Hero Boy, he performed for the motion-capture imagery. Tom Hanks, the film's lead, played the adult Hero Boy. Michelle told an interviewer that Josh was in good hands in the animation project. His 'facial expressions and body movements' would be captured by digital cameras, she said, referring to the pioneering techniques being used. She was confident that the film's well-respected producer and director Robert L. Zemeckis would weave great magic for the final version. 'Leave it to Zemeckis,' she said. 'He's out there. He always does the newest stuff.' The interviewer recalls Josh being hugely excited about the part. 'I supposedly fall off a train, and grab onto the back of it, and slingshot myself back up onto some guy's shoulders, and then we fell off again,' he told Crushable.

The next role he landed was a standout moment in his career trajectory. It was a part in the 2005 movie *Little Manhattan*, in which he would play alongside Charlie Ray. This romantic comedy gave him the chance to be involved in an eventual big-screen project from an early stage. 'It was really cool because I was involved with this movie before it became a movie,' he told TV.com. He was also thrilled by the choice of who would play his co-star. 'They were still developing the script and everything. I was there to read with all the different girls, and I got to have my opinion on which girl. Yeah, the thing is, I said that Charlie was one of my favourites, so that was really cool. I was so shocked when I found out that was her first audition ever because she was really so good.'

As was Josh. The film's director Mark Levin says that, at the auditions, Josh blew him and his colleagues away. Josh was the first hopeful they met at the reading and he made it 'impossible' for the crew to turn him away, said Levin. 'Josh is so game for anything that you put in front of him,' he continued. 'He's got an amazing acting style, which is that he is just "Johnny on the spot". You just say, "Hit that window," and he says "How hard?" And he does it again and again. And he enjoys it, he's just having fun . . . it's just kind of indicative of his incredible commitment.'

Having had his first real-life kiss at the age of eleven, during the shooting of *Little Manhattan* he had his first on-screen smooch. He was anxious about this scene and confided in director Levin. More than anything, Josh told the director, he could not quite understand why Ray did not share his nerves. Why was she not more apprehensive? As TV.com reported, Levin smiled and replied: 'Well, it's because girls mature faster than boys.' It was a useful lesson in acting and in life for young Josh.

Kentucky-raised chick: Jennifer beams at the camera in various school yearbook snaps.

(*above left*) Liam with his mother Leonie at the Cosmopolitan Fun Fearless Awards, 2010.
(*above right*) With older brothers Chris and Luke at an event in 2013.
(*below*) We are family: at the premiere of *Thor* with (l-r) Luke, Luke's wife Samantha, Chris, mum Leonie and dad Craig.

(*above left*) A young Josh attends the *Hansel & Gretel* premiere in 2002.
(*above right*) Still a cutie: Josh in his school yearbook photo, 2008.
(*below*) With brother Connor at the premiere of *Little Manhattan* in New York in 2005.

Young stars: *(above)* Jennifer with the cast of *The Bill Engvall Show* in 2007; *(below)* a young Josh stars in *Little Manhattan* with Charlie Ray.

(*above left*) Josh poses with his co-stars Kristen Stewart and
Jonah Bobo at the premiere of *Zathura: A Space Adventure* in 2005.
(*above right*) At 20th Century Fox's 'Adopt-a-Fire-House' event in
celebration of the release of *Firehouse Dog*, 2007.
(*below*) Starring alongside Robin Williams in *RV*, 2006.

Let the games commence!: *(above left)* Jennifer with her highschool cheerleading squad; *(above right)* Fresh-faced Jen strolls around New York; *(below and inset)* Liam and brother Chris attend the Oakley Learn to Ride event in Utah, 2011.

(above) Josh (top row, third from left) with team Nomar at the 3rd Annual Mia Hamm & Nomar Garciaparra Celebrity Soccer Challenge in California, 2010. (below left) Hangtime: Josh at the NBA All-Star Celebrity game in Houston; (below right) shooting some hoops at the 'Straight But Not Narrow' benefit game, both 2013.

(above) Liam signs autographs for fans as he arrives at the Australian Nickelodeon Kids' Choice Awards in 2010.
(below left) Liam poses with his co-hosts of the same event.
(below right) Josh onstage at The 23rd Annual GLAAD Media Awards in Los Angeles, 2012.

The conceit of the film is a love story told through the eyes of two eleven-year-old sweethearts. Josh plays the little adult role well. 'The story is not for those with a weak stomach,' announces his character with comic gravitas in the film's trailer. 'There's violence, heartache, cruelty,' he continues, 'but I'm going to tell it because someone has to tell the truth about love.' The film is full of memorable scenes. A standout Josh moment comes when he practises his chat-up lines in front of a mirror. As he stands, gazing at his own reflection while uttering punchlines such as: 'Hey there, pretty lady', he is almost like a much younger, much sweeter version of the Robert De Niro character Travis Bickle, whose iconic 'You talkin' to me?' line in *Taxi Driver* is also said to a mirror.

But his overall effect is more like a young Michael Cera, complete with the endearing awkwardness. There is a fair dose of physical humour in the film, including a comic moment when, just as Josh's character decides it is time to play it cool in front of the girl, he manages to walk straight into a glass door. He is also roundly beaten at karate, which throws up its own funny insights. Alongside him in the film were Cynthia Nixon, who plays his on-screen mother, popular star of *The West Wing* Bradley Whitford, who plays his on-screen father and – in just a momentary cameo – Josh's real brother Connor. Although Connor does not want to enter the entertainment industry, he took a role as a vomiting school boy in the film as a bit of fun – a taster of his big brother's exciting, strange world. Nixon was impressed with the elder Hutcherson, saying: 'Sometimes you just run across kids who are so grown-up. Josh is cute, but he is also smart and makes good choices.' Indeed, a side theme of the film could be a send-up of the fact that twenty-first-century American children sometimes mature at almost terrifying rates.

The critical community was impressed, with the BBC even going as far as positioning the film as a mini-Woody Allen effort. Stella Papamichael was praising of Josh, writing: 'Josh Hutcherson is a delight as the angst-ridden mini-urbanite who struggles to get his head around this thing called love.' Later in her write-up, she returned to our boy, with some phenomenal praise. 'Hutcherson's delivery is spot-on, showing a keen instinct for self-effacing humour that would make even Woody Allen feel that bit more inadequate,' she said.

Although Kevin Thomas, for the *Los Angeles Times*, was scathing of aspects of the film's script, he enjoyed the overall package, describing it as 'a handsome charmer about the avalanche of first love . . . an endearing, affectionately humorous and even lyrical depiction of the dawning of adolescence amid the privileged'. *Variety*, though, put a boot into young Josh, with its columnist Brian Lowry saying the boy 'might have looked cute on the page, but even with his Linus voice the language and tone don't feel natural'. Later, he sided with Josh against the film-makers, who he felt 'do their star no favours by saddling him with reams of stilted dialogue and a truly misguided scene where he must sob uncontrollably'.

The more biting of these comments were reminders that Josh had entered a very tough and very adult industry. However, as much as his family and others around him strove to protect him from the pain of rejection, criticism and other negative forces, ultimately he would have to come to terms with them for as long as he remained an actor. His skin was thickening – and it really had to, because any sense that critics and casting crews might have been wearing kid gloves would soon disappear as Josh got older.

Still, there remained plenty of childlike fun to be had. His next film was every boy actor's dream: a science-fiction space adventure. *Zathura: A Space Adventure* was, he recalled, 'awesome' thanks to the 'stunts and the cool way they filmed it'. Shot over three separate sets, the making of the movie gave Josh oodles of fun. 'One [set] shook like a 9.2 earthquake, one tilted at a forty-five-degree angle, and the other was still. Also, it was all in one place, so once we got there we got to do cool stuff with the trailer for Halloween and Christmas and stuff like that,' he told TV.com, his thrills palpable. 'It was a lot of fun.'

After the kid-like thrills and spills of working on *Zathura*, there was a more grown-up sense to his next project – at least that was what his mother Michelle was hoping. She was conscious of a need to define him as just an actor, as opposed to, specifically, a child actor. To this end she was delighted when Josh was selected to star alongside comedy acting legend Robin Williams in *RV: Runaway Vacation*. Josh played Carl, the son to Williams's company executive father Bob. The family (which also includes a mother played by Cheryl Hines and daughter played by JoJo Levesque) embark on a holiday that contains many surprises and, ultimately, familial redemption.

As for Josh, he recalls the movie was more about fun than about career advancement. He was just thrilled to be starring alongside a man he saw as a comic genius. 'Working with Robin is like watching him do stand-up constantly,' said Josh, who harboured his own comedic ambitions, as we have seen. 'It was so unbelievable to watch him do amazing improvisation,' he told TV.com. 'What was fun was getting to improv along with him because I love to do that, and the fact that I got to do it with Robin Williams still blows my mind.'

Having dreamed in younger years of becoming a stand-up comedian, Josh loved just being in the presence of Williams.

He has also spoken of the 'fun' he had working with 'the amazing cast'. Showing he was learning the ropes when it came to predictable movie-world tributes, he added: 'We got along so well, and since it was on location, we all did tons of stuff together away from the set and became great friends.' Safe, anodyne and backslapping, these were perfectly pitched words of praise from the young actor. His tone was in contrast to much of the reception for the film. Despite it starring Williams, who is popular among the media folk, it was widely lambasted. *Variety* said it suffered from 'blunt predictability and meagre laughs'. It also won unwelcome awards, including a Golden Raspberry for a special category called 'Worst Excuse for Family Entertainment'. However, Josh came within a whisker of a positive gong when he was nominated for a Young Artist Award in the wordy 'Best Performance in a Feature Film – Leading Young Actor' category. Having salvaged that from *RV*, Josh had better times just around the corner. His next film would be far more positively received and would lead to that all-important 'breakthrough' word.

The concerns that Chris and Michelle had felt over Josh's desire to enter the movie world were not unfounded. Some industry professionals are both outright exploitative and disingenuous. However, there are many diamonds among them. Josh has had a knack of discovering those diamonds wherever they lie and, during the making of the 2007 fantasy drama *Bridge to Terabithia*, Josh made a special friend. His co-star, AnnaSophia Robb was to capture his imagination to such an extent that it is fair to say she changed his life. The pair spent a lot of time together during the shooting in New Zealand, and Josh wondered how it was that they 'didn't get sick of each other', he told Movie Freak. During rare days off during the film-making the two youngsters 'took long rides in the country', said Josh, 'and hung out a lot'. As a pair of Americans surrounded by Kiwis, they developed a certain affinity. 'I think it shows in the film,' he said.

In the Walt Disney film, which is based on the Katherine Paterson novel of the same name, Josh plays a boy called Jess Aarons, who embarks on an initially unlikely friendship with a new girl on the block. They conjure up a fantasy world together, in a style reminiscent of Josh's own, real-life childhood creativities. The pair spend many an hour in a treehouse, continuing to develop their fantasy world, in which they rule as monarchs. Josh had initially been against the idea of taking on the character of Jess, as having read the novel he was unimpressed by how the character treated his younger sibling. His character's younger sister is played by Bailee Madison. As far as Josh is concerned, she almost became a real-life sister to him; such was the affection they developed for one another. He rates her as an amazing talent and recalls the day he saw her crying off-set. He asked her what was wrong and she replied that she was merely gearing herself up for an emotional scene she was about to film. Josh decided she was the most grown-up little person he'd ever met. Indeed, he said that he was so struck by her that he wondered if he would ever meet anyone quite like her in his entire life.

There was such fun to be had, though he was unsure of a couple of the outfits he had to wear on set. One he felt made him look as if he were wearing a kilt. The crown he wore in the film's emotional climax made him look like 'some sort of monk or something', he told TV.com.

However, he loved the action scenes in which he got to 'fight the creatures in the forest'. Here, he had to really use his imagination to make his acting authentic. 'I have a pretty good imagination and now I have a bit of experience in the business and you learn things,' he said. He still found it hard, though he hoped that any boys who went to watch the film would have loved these scenes as much as he did. The scenes in which his character cries were the ones that many females identified with.

The film itself attracted plentiful praise – as did Josh's part in it. The *Washington Post* swept away the negative feelings left by Empire's questioning over Josh's part in *Runaway Vacation* by describing him, in this movie, as 'perfectly cast'. The *Village Voice* loved how Josh portrayed the 'sensitive, artistic temperament' of his character. The *Chicago Sun-Times* was unequivocal: 'Ultimately, the film's heart and soul rests on the abilities of its young lead characters to make us really see the world through children's eyes. The dynamic duo of Hutcherson and Robb do not disappoint.' Josh also won an award, finally landing the gong for which he had been nominated after his previous outing: the Best Performance in a Feature Film – Leading Young Actor at the Young Artist Awards. In all, the film and its cast was nominated for seven major honours, of which it won five.

Commercially, it was surprisingly successful. 'Nobody really expected that,' Josh told Movie Freak. He said that people thought it would do 'okay', but no better. Most significant for him was that the film had transported him from the realms of the cinematic sidelines to a more central place. Where his crying scenes in *Little Manhattan* had included a helping of humour, his sobbing scenes here were entirely serious and emotional affairs.

The way he nailed them stunned Gábor Csupó, the film's director, who said he thought Josh was 'amazing'. Csupó confirmed that these were genuine teardrops, not 'CGI or anything', adding: 'he really melted into this performance'.

Josh is proud of how he fared, and well he may be. 'I really did cry in the movie,' he told Collider. 'It's what you have to do when you're in character.' He said that his approach to such challenging requirements had already evolved. In earlier years he would force the tears out by imagining something genuinely sad in his own life. 'But now, what I do is just really get into my character,' he said. 'If it's a situation where my character would cry, then I just think like I am them and make myself cry.'

Next up, quite a different proposition was put on the table for Josh. When he was offered a part in a dog movie, he was not sure what to say at first. The world of film is peppereed with formulaic, syrupy canine movies – would this one have anything original about it? He felt reassured when he read the script. 'For some reason it had such a great feel to me,' he told the *Lexington Herald-Leader*. 'It was unlike any other dog movie, because it had such a cool storyline. It was so different to any other dog movie I had ever seen or ever heard of. That's what really attracted me to it – that it was so unique.' The film was *Firehouse Dog* – another family flick for his already-crowded resumé.

Directed by Todd Holland, the film tells the story of Shane Fahey – played by Josh – and his relationship with a dog who has been miraculously rescued from a burning building. The dog, called Rexx, turns out to secretly be a celebrity mutt who has starred in movies. Four different dogs played Rexx, giving Josh plenty of chance for off-screen bonding with man's best friend. The only problem with this was that his real-life pet, a boxer dog called Diesel, got envious and possessive. 'I was spending so much time on set with the other dog that he was like, "Hey man, what's up? What's going on?"' The biggest challenge in this film was a scene in which he was trapped by fire and had to take an axe to a door. He choked on set as he adjusted to the smoky conditions.

The critics were, in parts, harsh on the film – but most were positive about Josh. *Variety* called the movie 'likeable but ungainly'; though more pertinent to Josh was that the influential magazine also identified him as 'fast becoming the studios' go-to guy for sensitive, neglected tykes'. The *Boston Post*, too, liked Josh more than the film itself: 'Hutcherson has enough built-in soul to make Shane's emotional journey from grumpy to cheerful believable,' it declared. Less abashed was the *Philadelphia Inquirer*, which said Josh was 'emerging as the Jodie Foster of Generation Y. (With his crooked grin and spray of freckles, he even looks enough like Foster to be mistaken for her son.) With each successive film Hutcherson dives deeper into his reservoir of shame and hurt and hope, unnerving for one so young, but also unusually urgent for an actor of any age.'

He could ill afford to let such praise go to his head. Thanks to his parents and advisers, he managed to stay more grounded than many. The ongoing challenge for him was to keep growing in all senses. Being a 'go-to guy' for particular roles was a fine achievement. Like nearly all actors, though, success in one domain only spurred Josh on to want to conquer others. That restless, unquenchable feeling was what drove him on, and still does, even following the success of *The Hunger Games*. Indeed, it is fair to say that the heroes of Hollywood survive on their hunger. A more adult and 'credible' opportunity gave him a bite-sized sense of satisfaction in the form of *Winged Creatures*, the crime flick directed by Rowan Woods. Josh's role – a kid called Jimmy Jaspersen – was a minor one, but his involvement with the film gave a nice lick of edge to his filmography. The film was later released on DVD with the new title, *Fragments*.

Josh hopped straight back to the mainstream in *Journey to the Center of the Earth*. In this 3-D science fantasy blockbuster, his level of public recognition rocketed. The film took $20 million on its opening weekend alone. A modern adaptation of a 1950s classic, *Journey* saw Josh play Sean Anderson, who joins his father and a tour guide on a journey to the planet's core. Ahead of the making of the film, Josh purposefully eschewed the option of watching the original movie, or reading the novel on which it was based. This was part of a deliberate and wider policy of his. 'I like to go into each project with a fresh mind,' he told the Film School Rejects site. Only once the film was made did he feel ready to study the originals. 'Everybody's telling me it's an amazing book and I love the story. I lived it, so I've gotta definitely check it out.'

In promoting *Journey*, Josh indirectly reminded the world that for all his poise he was still a fifteen-year-old boy. 'It's really good,' said Josh. 'It's a cliff-hanger kind of story.' He loved the 'action' and 'excitement' of it all, including the scenes in which they were forced to escape from flowing lava. Working in front of 'green screen' special effects again, he continued to learn fast. 'You have to ad lib. You are staring at a mark on the wall. It is more technical and more tedious. You have to pretend that you are being chased by a giant albino dinosaur.' Again, Josh's inherently strong imagination paid dividends.

He had to consume some rather peculiar

concoctions in the film, including the drool of a dinosaur. 'It was like that stuff you put on your sunburns afterwards, that gel stuff, mixed with balsa wood and cork,' he told Film School Rejects. 'At least that's what they told me it was. It tasted like crap. But it wasn't hazardous, so that's the good news.' When he had to eat arthropod guts, again the mixture was . . . interesting. 'It was like chicken salad and milk, mixed together with some sort of really sour stuff in it. So it was really not that tasty. It was a gag effect for real, totally.' However, he loved *Journey*, describing it as 'my most favourite and most fun movie to work on and to watch'. Indeed, for the foreseeable future at least, he decided on action movies as his preferred genre. 'As of now, that's one of my favourite genres just because I'm young and I get to do all the stunts and fun stuff,' he said.

Meanwhile, life outside of Josh's work commitments continued apace, and new adventures included learning to drive. He tried to keep his life as normal as he could. 'When I'm not filming movies I love being home and getting to do normal kid things with my friends,' he said. He was aiming to keep as true as possible to his parents' long-standing wish for him to remain as grounded and normal as possible, even as his fame increased. He had fewer opportunities to read than he would have liked, yet when he did find the time to sit down with a book his choices sometimes raised eyebrows. He loved to read about subjects as heavy as theoretical physics and philosophy. 'I like the deeper "What does it mean to be a person?", "What is reality?", "What is a consciousness?","How is it we can ask these kinds of questions?",' he told TeenHollywood. 'That's what I want to know.'

As well as satisfying his emotional and spiritual curiosity, these explorations also helped him to better understand characters in his films. As for himself, he felt that he was a blend between a Kentucky kid and a Hollywoodian. 'I feel like I have a mix of both Kentucky and LA. Literally half of my life, since I was nine years old, I've been going back and forth between Kentucky and Los Angeles, spending the majority of my time in LA,' he said. But he was certain he had lived 'a very normal life, even though I've been making movies since I was nine'.

He began dating and soon developed gripes about certain behaviour during such encounters. 'Checking your phone a lot is a big pet peeve of mine,' he said. If a girl did that it made him wonder if he was boring her, which is never a nice feeling. There was also an old-fashioned technophobe at work in this. 'I'm not very into technology. I'm not on the Internet that much. I'm not all over Twitter or Facebook, so I'm very analog. I prefer a date to be more analog,' he told TeenHollywood. As for his tastes in women, they are varied. 'I like both athletic girls and girlie girls,' he said, though added he would not want one so sporty that she could better him on the field. He also says he likes 'girls I can have deep conversations with', as opposed to girls who 'play the ditzy dumb thing', he told Hollywood Life. That sort of behaviour, he says, makes him think 'Oh, God, please stop!'

He was linked with a young lady called Shannon Wada, who had dreams of becoming a famous actress and model, and to whom he was introduced by a mutual friend. He has also been linked with the actress Vanessa Hudgens, who first rose to prominence playing Gabriella Montez in the *High School Musical* franchise. She dated her co-star Zac Efron for a while, their relationship capturing the imagination of the public so much that they became known collectively as 'Zanessa', in the style of 'Brangelina'. When Josh starred opposite the glamorous Hudgens in *Journey 2: The Mysterious Island*, the media could scarcely contain their hopes that another relationship would be sparked, following Hudgens's break-up with Efron.

In response to one of many media questions about whether they were dating, Josh was coy. 'Oh, boy, I don't know if "dating" is the right word,' he told *Seventeen*. 'She's awesome. We love being together. When I first met her, we just really hit it off. We could be goofy and silly and not worry about anything except having fun. I adore her.' Later, after they had split, he was again evasive. 'We're not,' he said when asked if they were dating by the Australian morning television show *Today*, as he sat slightly uncomfortably alongside Hudgens. 'We were at one point, but she broke my heart. No, I'm just kidding, that was a while ago, we're really good friends now.' The *Huffington Post* deemed it 'the most awkward interview ever'. As for Hudgens, she had previously told Ellen DeGeneres: 'Yes, I'm single. Can't a girl have friends?'

Josh remained ever vigilant and mindful of the need to manage his transformation from child actor to actor. As he explained to TeenHollywood, it was the movie *The Kids Are All Right* that, more than any, helped him across that invisible but crucial divide. 'I've always wanted to choose my roles carefully because of that,' he said. 'When I first started acting I was in love with it. I knew I wanted to do it all my life so making that transition from a child star into an adult actor has always been on my mind. I think it's just happened naturally over the years as I've gotten older. My work has spoken for itself and I've been able to do movies like *The Kids Are All Right*, that kind of aged me up a little bit. I think that was one of the bigger ones that pushed me into a different category.'

The Kids Are All Right was, in terms of plot, a million miles from some of the more wholesome stories in which he had previously appeared. Yet, in its essence, it had themes that chimed with *Little Manhattan* and *Runaway Vacation*: family and love. In the film, Josh played Laser, the son of two lesbian mothers and sibling of Joni. When the man who was sperm donor for both children suddenly shows up in their lives, much drama, confusion, comedy and warmth ensues. 'Laser is a teen who's trying to figure out who he is and how he fits into the world, and I know I identified with that,' Josh said. Which teenager would not? 'The story was so real and it encapsulated the family and depicted it in a way that has never been done before, and I loved it,' he continued. 'As an actor I feel like a lot of times your job is to portray real life or the complete opposite, a fantastical world. I've done a lot of fantastical crazy stuff that doesn't exist, so to break it down into something that was so real and genuine like this was really fun and different.' It was also a shorter process than some of his other films: *Zathura* was a ninety-three-day shoot, while *The Kids* was just twenty-three. 'I loved it,' he said of the experience. 'The intimacy that you get with an independent film like this is unlike a studio film. The collaboration and the creative freedom that you have is really nice.'

He found it fairly easy to build a convincing bond

with Mia Wasikowska, despite their having little time ahead of filming – and little during the shooting – to get to know each other. 'Mia has a younger brother who's about my age, and I have a brother, so for us to jump into the sibling roles it's a similar situation,' Josh told Cinema Blend. The key to making it click was, he added, a certain degree of sheer confidence and faith. 'You just sort of have to leap and not look sometimes and go for it and have no inhibitions and not be shy,' he said. The film worked for the critics – and so did Josh. The *Patriot Ledger* described Josh's performance as 'effortless'. 'The kids really are all right in *The Kids Are All Right*', cheered the *Miami Herald*. 'The cast are phenomenal,' said the Ultra Culture website. Several journals awarded it their 'film of the year' honour.

Josh had gathered credibility aplenty with this film, though another film he took part in around the same time was not such a happy outing. In *Cirque du Freak: The Vampire's Assistant*, he played Steve, who he described as a 'vampaneze – which is basically an evil vampire'. He loved playing Steve, who he summed up as a 'reckless type'. What he really enjoyed was the chance to play 'a bad guy kind of role'. Or more specifically, as he put it in an interview with Film School Rejects, 'I was a sucker [rather than a suckee].' Having watched and loved old-fashioned films such as *Interview with the Vampire* and *The Lost Boys*, he found the whole vampire adventure a joy.

But the film was savaged by many of the critics and drew far less at the box office than anyone involved had hoped. The expectation that the film would be as popular as the *Twilight* saga, but with a fan base of boys as well as girls, proved overly optimistic. At least the *Chicago Reader* had written glowingly of the 'hell-raising Josh Hutcherson', proving he had broadened his image in these unfamiliar cinematic pastures. 'It's cool to play a vampire,' said an unabashed Josh. 'Vampires can do whatever they want whenever they want, like fly around all the time. Plus, girls like vampires. Maybe they don't want to admit it, but they do, which is a plus.'

So there we have Josh Hutcherson, as he stood on the brink of the part that would propel him to his highest point yet. The success the gentle young man had enjoyed had not come without hard work. Indeed, from the earliest years of his life he had needed to strive to win over his first 'tough audience': that of his parents. They had always been proud of their son's ability to entertain – they just wondered whether it was really appropriate for him to make a career out of it. But if he had proved himself prior to *The Hunger Games*, he would do so again.

PART TWO

———

LIFE AFTER THE GAMES

Chapter Seven

LET THE GAMES COMMENCE!

Inspiration for novels can strike in all sorts of strange circumstances. J. K. Rowling conjured up the idea for the *Harry Potter* series while sitting on a delayed train. This alone suggests that boredom can be the mother of invention, just as much as necessity can. Stephenie Meyer, on the other hand, was inspired to write the *Twilight* series after a dream-filled night's sleep. George Orwell was moved to write *Animal Farm* when he watched a farm boy pulling a cart.

The idea for *The Hunger Games* came about one evening, as author Suzanne Collins was sitting watching television, the remote control in her hand. As she flicked between various channels, she was struck by a curious juxtaposition: reality television contests and news footage of fighting in Iraq. The combination set her thinking and her rich imagination began to whizz into action. The result was a story she would eventually call *The Hunger Games*. It would change her life – and then the lives of Jennifer, Liam and Josh.

Collins had been forming the framework of the story all her life. The personality and imagination that created District 12 were shaped throughout her childhood in America and Europe. She was raised in a family rich in militaristic heritage. Her grandfather was gassed while fighting in the First World War, while her uncle sustained shrapnel wounds in the Second World War. Most pertinently, she was reared by the most military-minded of fathers. Michael was an Air Force officer who served in the Vietnam War. Collins was six years of age when her father left to serve overseas. It was a departure which cut her deeply: as she later told the *New York Times*, she used to worry about him and wonder when he was coming home to Indiana. 'As time passes and the absence is longer and longer, you become more and more concerned – but you don't really have the words to express your concern,' she said. 'There's only this continued absence.'

Her dad was also a historian, military specialist and a doctor of political science. Indeed, one of her earliest childhood memories is of young men in uniform at West Point, where her father was teaching army history. Military matters were therefore a feature of her childhood in a way that was rare, thanks to her father's background and ongoing interest. After he returned from Vietnam, he moved the family to Brussels. There, the young Collins and her three siblings were taken by their father to visit various famous historical battlefields in Europe and given frank lectures on the conflicts that were fought there, including technical details and discussion of the moral dimensions of it all. Michael weaved a vivid and compelling narrative. 'You didn't just stand there,' said Collins to Scholastic. 'You would hear what led up to this war and to this particular battle, what transpired there, and what the fallout was. It wasn't like, there's a field. It would be, here's a story.'

Warfare and storytelling: these were the dual influences on her life during her childhood and adolescence, thanks to her father. Another adult whose childhood influence on Collins helped bring *The Hunger Games* about was her English teacher, Miss Vance. Collins remembers how, during her fifth- and sixth-grade years, Miss Vance used to take a set of tale-loving pupils to one side and read them stories written by nineteenth-century American author Edgar Allan Poe. 'I remember all of us sitting around just wide-eyed as she read "The Tell-Tale Heart" or "The Mask of the Red Death",' said Collins during an interview with the Scholastic website. 'She didn't think we were too young to hear it. And we were riveted. That made a huge impression on me.'

Completing the circle was Suzanne's childhood fascination with the tales of Greek mythology: in particular, the story of Theseus and the Minotaur. 'I was a huge fan of Greek and Roman mythology,' she told the *School Library Journal*. 'The story took my breath away because it was so cruel and Crete was so ruthless,' she said. 'The message is: "Mess with us and we'll do something worse than kill you – we'll kill your children." And the thing is, it was allowed; the parents sat by powerless to stop it.' She went on to describe Katniss as a 'futuristic Theseus'. Another influence on Collins was the legendary gladiator Spartacus, who, she identified, 'follows the same arc from slave to gladiator to rebel to face of war'.

While these influences formed the backdrop of a story set in an era of reality television and international conflicts, the scene was ready for Collins to create something truly stunning. It took someone with her background, her timing and, most of all, her vision to make this happen. First, though, she had to complete her apprenticeship as a writer, so her pen could be as sharp as possible when she turned to the concept that underpins *The Hunger Games* series.

Her first foray into writing came in the shape of a children's novel called *Gregor the Overlander*. Naturally, there is a warfare theme to the tale, which is about an eleven-year-old boy called Gregor. He and his sister fall through a grate in the ground and discover a subterranean world of rats, spiders and cockroaches. He tries to free himself and his sister from this scary world until he discovers that their presence there has been foretold in a prophecy. What happens next changes his life and the subterranean world for ever. The novel hit the stores in 2003 and the publisher, Scholastic, soon bought the rights to the rest of the series. The final book in the series was a *New York Times* bestseller. Collins has also written for television. She is behind children's shows that have been shown on PBS and Nickelodeon. Her projects, some of which have been nominated for prestigious Emmy Awards, include *Oswald*, *Little Bear* and *Clifford's Puppy Days*.

These projects had given her considerable success. Yet it was *The Hunger Games* series that would change her life, and bring Jennifer, Liam and Josh directly into it. The longer she worked on *The Hunger Games*, Collins became more convinced that the overall project carried with it considerable responsibility. She felt that the story would actually provide a public service for a generation. 'It's crucial that young readers are considering scenarios about humanity's future, because the challenges are about to land on their laps,' she told the *New York Times*. 'I hope they question how elements of the books might be relevant in their own lives. About global warming, about our mistreatment of the environment, but also questions like: how do you feel about the fact that some people take their next meal for granted when so many other people are starving in the world?'

Warming to her social theme, she continued: 'What do you think about choices your government, past and present, or other governments around the world make? What's your relationship to reality TV versus your relationship to news?' She went on to encourage younger readers to reflect on anything in the book that disturbed them because it reminded them of something in their own life. If anything did resonate with them that way, she said, they might reflect on what they could do to change it. 'Because you know what? Even if they're not of your making, these issues and how to deal with them become your responsibility.'

In common with many of Collins's everyday readers, Jennifer Lawrence certainly sees parallels between the fiction of the movie and the fact of the real world. 'The Hunger Games is not that far off from real life,' she told Seventeen. 'We are living in a world where we watch extreme sports shows where people get hurt or killed. It takes a lot to shock us.' The exploitation of reality television is something that fiction writers are increasingly turning to. For instance, in Channel 4's dark drama series Black Mirror, Charlie Brooker came up with a sinister spoof of The X Factor and similar shows. Here, the cruelty and exploitation that many pundits see underlying such series were exaggerated and laid bare. It made for uncomfortable viewing. Other television series and books have also poked fun at and asked serious questions of the genre, yet few have done so quite so imaginatively as The Hunger Games.

No wonder, then, that, upon publication, the first book quickly became a commercial and critical success, climbing straight to the top of the bestseller lists. Reviewers, with few exceptions, practically scrapped to produce the most glowing tribute to the book. Time magazine said it was 'a chilling, bloody and thoroughly horrifying book'. Even Twilight author Stephenie Meyer, who might have felt threatened by the series, came out as a fan, declaring herself 'obsessed'. The New York Times foreshadowed the importance of Jennifer's part in the film when it declared: 'the considerable strength of the novel comes in Collins's convincingly detailed world-building and her memorably complex and fascinating heroine'.

Stephen King offered a mixed verdict in his review of it for *Entertainment Weekly*. He said *The Hunger Games* was a 'violent, jarring speed-rap of a novel that generates nearly constant suspense and may also generate a fair amount of controversy', adding, 'I couldn't stop reading'. He described Collins as 'an efficient no-nonsense prose stylist with a pleasantly dry sense of humour' and her book as 'addictive'. However, he said that there were 'displays of authorial laziness that kids will accept more readily than adults'. One should factor in to this criticism that King had been merciless in the past about the *Twilight* books, declaring loftily during an interview with *USA Weekend* that author Meyer 'can't write worth a darn'.

Yet despite its commercial and, mostly, critically stunning success, the publication of *The Hunger Games* was not without controversy. It was suggested by some that there was evidence of plagiarism in the storyline, with critics identifying what they see as similarities between Collins's work and the 2000 Japanese novel *Battle Royale*. The latter title, written by Koushun Takami, is set in a dystopian future in which a tyrannical government forces teenagers to fight to the death in a televised contest. It was developed into a film, which was described by Quentin Tarantino as his 'favourite movie of the last twenty years'. The plagiarism allegation was a serious one: it is, perhaps, the worst thing of which a fiction writer can be accused.

Collins, naturally, came out fighting. She insisted that she had not plagiarized *Battle Royale*, telling the *New York Times*: 'I had never heard of that book or that author until my book was turned in. At that point, it was mentioned to me, and I asked my editor if I should read it. He said: "No, I don't want that world in your head. Just continue what you're doing."' Yet once word got out on the Internet that there were perceptions of plagiarism, Collins's work was, as the *New York Times* put it, 'savaged on the blogosphere as a bald-faced rip-off'. While fans of each novel embarked on passionate online wars defending their respective author's honour, the author of *Battle Royale* was far more laid back about the affair. Though Takami told ABC News he appreciated his fans 'standing up' for his book, he declined to be drawn into the controversy itself. 'I think every novel has something to offer,' Takami wrote in an email to the news division. 'If readers find value in either book, that's all an author can ask for.'

Plagiarism allegations have struck the authors of

several recent successful young adult novel series. J. K. Rowling was accused by the estate of author Adrian Jacobs of plagiarizing parts of Jacobs's novel *The Adventures of Willy the Wizard*. Rowling told the BBC the claim was 'not only unfounded but absurd', adding that she had not even read *The Adventures* until the claim was launched in 2004. A six-year battle broke out, which ended in 2011 when a court case against Rowling failed. Lawyers representing author Jordan Scott claimed that *Breaking Dawn*, of Stephenie Meyer's smash-hit *Twilight* series, showed 'a striking and substantial similarity' to Scott's book *The Nocturne*. Meyer's publisher, Hachette, responded with a statement that said that neither Meyer nor her representatives 'had any knowledge of this writer or her supposed book prior to this claim'. Meyer herself has rigorously denied the suggestion.

Collins was shaken by the row but, having again strongly denied it, was looking forward to facilitating a cinematic adaptation of her work as film companies began to circle. Several big-hitters were desperate to put *The Hunger Games* on the big screen. The deal went to the movie house Lionsgate, which was hungry for a big success after a series of disappointing films. Over the previous two years, its movies *Killers*, *Conan the Barbarian* and *Warrior* fell far short of expectation at the box office. The

(above) Jennifer poses with her Marcello Mastroianni prize for her role in *The Burning Plane* at the 65th Venice International Film Festival, 2008. (below) At the 2010 Film Independent's Screening of *Winter's Bone*, the film for which she was first Oscar-nominated.

(above) A scene from *The Last Song*; Liam and Miley's onscreen chemistry would be mirrored in real life.
(below left) The pair attend the World Premiere of *The Last Song* in Hollywood in 2010.
(below right) Young love: taking an off-duty stroll around LA.

(above) Jennifer and *X-Men* co-star Nicholas Hoult attend Amber Lounge Fashion Monaco in 2012.
(below left) A more casual affair: the pair are spotted out and about in London's Soho in 2012.
(below right) Josh is believed to have had a brief romance with his *Journey 2* co-star Vanessa Hudgens.

(above) Eddie Hassell, Julianne Moore, Mia Wasikowska, Josh and Mark Ruffalo attend *The Kids Are All Right* premiere at the 2010 Sundance Film Festival.
(below left) A serious chat: Liam attends the afterparty of the US premiere of *Paranoia* with Harrison Ford in 2013.
(below right) Jennifer at the 20th Century Fox Presentation at 2013 Comic-Con with her fellow *X-Men* star Patrick Stewart.

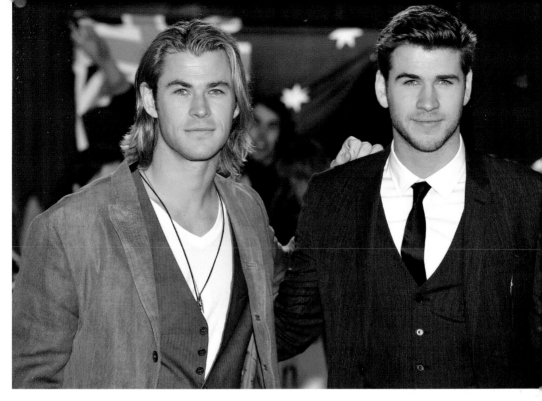

(above) Brothers in arms: Liam with brother Chris at the London premiere of *The Hunger Games*, held at the O2 Arena.

(below) Josh soaks up the adoration of his fans as he visits New.Music.Live at MuchMusic HQ in Toronto, Canada.

(*above*) Liam, Jen and Josh sign merchandise for fans at *The Hunger Games* US Mall Tour Kick-Off in LA, 2012.
(*below left*) Glittering Jennifer and director Gary Ross attend the premiere of the film at the Nokia Theatre in LA.
(*below right*) Horsing around at the photocall for *Catching Fire* at Comic-Con, San Diego in 2013.

(above left) Jennifer and Bradley Cooper attend a special screening of *Silver Linings Playbook* presented by the Weinstein Company in 2012.
(above right) Alongside Anne Hathaway and clutching her Oscar for Best Actress at the 85th Academy Awards in 2013.
(below) At the Governors Ball with her family: brother Ben (left), mum Karen, dad Gary and brother Blaine (right).

Bright young things: the three stars are now known the world over . . . and this is only the beginning.

movie house had enjoyed several years of success thanks to the grotesquely brilliant *Saw* horror franchise, but with that series finished, it was keen for a new hit.

Nina Jacobson, who had worked on films that included *The Princess Diaries* and *The Pirates of the Caribbean* series, landed the job as producer after an impassioned pitch to Collins. Then, following some keen bidding, Gary Ross was given the plum job of director. 'I'm so touched by the humanity of Katniss,' Ross told *Entertainment Weekly* in typically Hollywood tones. 'As much as the firestorm or the final action sequences are incredibly riveting and enormous, it's the relationships in the books that are the most moving to me.' When news had first broken of his appointment, Ross's take on the films was echoed by fans. An eighth-grade reading teacher from Lubbock's Frenship Middle School told her 134 students to each compose a letter for the director with their personal advice on how to best direct this popular story. 'So many of them wrote "Listen, I know this is an action movie and I can't wait to see the action but please don't lose the heart of the story,"' said Ross.

Collins was delighted by how Ross went on to handle the screenplay. Authors often feel sick with nerves when they first clutch an adaptation of their own precious work. The scope for causing offence is huge. When she first read it she was hugely relieved and excited to see what he had done. 'I was like, "Oh my God, he found the emotional arc to the story,"' she told *Entertainment Weekly*. 'I saw in Gary's draft that it was the first time it had been successfully done as an overall arc. Without it you have a film, you have a story, but you risk losing the kind of emotional impact that the film might have.' Collins's role in the new project was clear, yet complicated by a need for concealment, as she continued. 'At the beginning, I attached myself as the first screenwriter,' she said. 'I was writing the third book and there was great secrecy about it and no one could know how it ended. But I knew that if the screenplay got off on the wrong foot, that you could end up with something by which you could never reach the events of the third book. And since I couldn't reveal information to the film team, I wanted to be around to keep an eye on that. After that, I didn't know.'

It was time for Jennifer, Liam and Josh to enter the process. For the all-important casting, there was a strong wave of opinion that Katniss's part should be given to an unknown actress, in order to preserve and even strengthen the feeling the fans of the books had that she was their character. 'I don't think she should be famous,' producer Nina Jacobson told *Entertainment Weekly*. 'I think that fans want Katniss to belong to them and I understand that. And I think that sometimes with people who have a strong other identity – as a celebrity or as a well known other character – you feel like that person doesn't belong to you and I think that's what fans are looking for.' Yet among those in the running for the part were, reportedly, *True Grit*'s Hailee Steinfeld, Chloë Moretz of *Kick-Ass* fame, and *Little Miss Sunshine*'s Abigail Breslin.

Jennifer, Liam and Josh each auditioned for their respective parts and then nervously waited for news of their success, or otherwise. Josh was so keen that he whipped the media into a frenzy when, as he waited for news, he told *Entertainment Weekly* how much he related to the role of Peeta. 'I love Peeta,' he said. 'The character is so much who I am – self-deprecating, a people person. And he'd be such a great character to play! Like in the third book? Oh my God.' He hoped to land the part, but was realistic, saying: 'But they're meeting a lot of people right now – one can only dream.' He had dreamed since he was a kid – but now he dreamt big.

Yet the tension was no less for his co-stars. For Jennifer, the waiting was particularly difficult. Her desire to succeed had only been boosted by the fact that she unsuccessfully auditioned for the part of Bella for the *Twilight* franchise. Having watched that series soar to enormous success, with Kristen Stewart taking the character on, Jennifer was all the keener to be part of *The Hunger Games*, a tweeny literary trilogy she could see being just as successful in the cinemas. Little could she know that, in fact, the moment her name was first mentioned in casting meetings it 'sent shivers up the spine' of producer Jon Kilik, so sure was he she would be perfect. Then, following Jennifer's *Hunger* audition, the film's director, Gary Ross, had told Lionsgate: 'Look, this comes along once every ten years.' As he put it later, 'Someone walks in the door with that kind of massive talent, it knocks you back in your chair.'

Jennifer had loved the books. Indeed, she had read them when she was preparing for an Oscars season. She particularly enjoyed the opportunity the inner dialogue offered Katniss for the big-screen version. She also felt that the novels ventured an 'ugly truth about our world', showing the brutality that all people have within them. 'I love that it's kind of this sick look at our world that's obsessed with reality TV and obsessed with brutality.' After she had auditioned, Jennifer told Ross that she would understand if she was not cast, and then gave a mini-pitch for the part, by talking to him about the character's complexities.

Liam was aware of the popularity of the books

before he turned to read them, but on doing so he was surprised, noting 'how dark and gritty the story was'. He wondered whether the scenario upon which *The Hunger Games* is based could one day come true. 'When you think about the fast-growing popularity of reality TV today, and the crazy premise of many of the reality-TV shows that are currently on the air, is it really that far off for us to consider something like this being possible?' he asked. 'I think it's a mind-blowing thing to think about.' The themes behind the novel, as well as the storyline itself, had gripped what would be the film version's leading trio.

In March 2011, Jennifer's waiting was finally over as Lionsgate confirmed the actress had won the role of Katniss. She was in London when she took the call and it came as quite a shock as she had convinced herself that she would not be offered the part. 'I was then terrified,' she said, describing the enormity of it all.

'Jennifer's just an incredible actress,' said Collins in a statement. 'So powerful, vulnerable, beautiful, unforgiving and brave. I never thought we'd find somebody this perfect for the role. And I can't wait for everyone to see her play it.' The author phoned Jennifer to tell her personally how pleased she was. She told the actress she felt that a great weight had been lifted from her shoulders thanks to her casting. She had seen, she later told *Entertainment Weekly*, 'a girl who has the potential rage to send an arrow into the Gamemakers, and the protectiveness to make Rue her ally'. She just felt instinctively that Jennifer could truly nail this part.

Then, a few weeks later, it was announced that Josh had landed the part of Peeta, and Liam had been cast as Gale. Josh had impressed everyone, with executive producer Robin Bissell declaring that, in the audition, 'immediately he was Peeta – I mean, it was that clear'. Jacobson felt the same, describing admiringly how Josh had 'really captured that Peeta-ocity' of the role. And as far as Collins was concerned, Josh gave an absolutely perfect audition for the part. 'You know people may get thrown, say, by the colour of an actor's hair or maybe something physical, but I tell you: if Josh had been bright purple and had had six-foot wings and gave that audition, I'd have been like "Cast him! We can work around the wings",' she told *Entertainment Weekly*. 'He was that good. That role is so key to have a boy that can use language. That's how Peeta navigates the world, that's his gift, and Josh was the one who could bring that to life in such a real and natural way.'

It must have been quite an audition, for Ross, speaking in the same interview, agreed: 'After the reading, we looked at each other, we didn't even have to say anything, because we both were like "Wow, that's it." Literally he walked out of the room and we high-fived.' Ross later compared Josh to 'a young Jack Lemmon', so impressed was he. Collins agreed with the overall praise. 'Every one of those kids earned those roles by virtue of the auditions they gave,' she said. 'Those three kids? They were all our first choice.' Nonetheless, Josh has admitted to MTV that he was 'on pins and needles waiting to find out' if he had been cast.

The crew were thrilled with Liam's audition, too. Nina admired Liam's reading for Gale, describing the actor as a 'big, hunky guy' who can 'communicate very effectively with his eyes and with the small gestures'. Liam had been up against strong talents including David Henrie, Chris Massoglia, Drew Roy and Robbie Amell for the part and he had beaten them all. The crew all noted how well Josh and Liam related to one another while acting. Everything looked great. When Josh learned he had got the part he sent a text to Liam saying: 'Dude, we have *The Hunger Games*! I'm so stoked, man. This is awesome!' As a joke, Liam pretended in his reply that he had not been so lucky. Their banter would continue throughout the making of the franchise.

Often, actors buy themselves a huge treat to

celebrate landing a plum part in a big film. But as Liam told Collider, this was not how he greeted the news and neither would it be in his style to do so. 'Honestly, I'm not an extravagant person, I don't spend a lot of money,' he said. 'Most of my money goes back to Australia for my older brother; I buy him gifts all the time and my parents. I don't spend a lot of money on myself, really.' Instead, he merely had a small celebratory party with some friends. He preferred to concentrate on preparation rather than indulgence.

The leading trio was complete, and each of the stars was thrilled to be on-board. Liam said that he felt the books were richly cinematic in style. 'You read it and you can just kind of see everything,' he said. 'I read the first book and I loved it. I didn't realize how good the writing was.' Jennifer had read the books before she knew she would one day audition for the movie. She told *Vanity Fair* that as she began work on the film she felt like 'a fan that gets to dress up'. Her mother Karen, too, read them and thought 'it was an incredible role and story'. Karen had also made the same call on *Winter's Bone*, so 'she must be a clairvoyant, or just . . . really good taste', she said. Josh, meanwhile, recalled that as he first read the books his 'mind was being blown' by how similar he felt to the character Peeta. 'I felt like I could relate,' he said.

Liam, though, was drawn to Gale who, he said, 'felt more right than Peeta'.

Jennifer might have felt like a fan but she also realized quickly that she was stepping into a character who meant an enormous amount to the book's legion of fans. Some were delighted to learn of her casting, others were not so sure. There were complaints that Jennifer was physically wrong to be Katniss – her hair too light and her eyes the wrong shade – and some also noted that at twenty-one, Jennifer was older than the quintessentially teenage character. As for Jennifer, she only learned of the complaints about her hair colour after she had dyed it brown for the part. She gave short shrift to the controversy, highlighting the apparent surprise of the fans that 'blonde hair can turn brown'. With the hair problem duly dealt with, she also noted wryly: 'So now is the only time that I'm being told that people hated me at first?' Make-up artist Ve Neill said Jennifer was 'stunning' with dark hair. In terms of make-up itself, Neill told *The Hunger Games Official Illustrated Movie Companion*, 'we wanted to keep her as natural as possible – beautiful and unaffected.'

There was also controversy that Jennifer and Liam's characters were, in the eyes of some fans of the novel, of mixed-race origin. Why, such readers wondered, were two white actors cast for the parts?

Was this an implicit suggestion on the part of the film-makers that mainstream audiences needed the cast 'whitened up' for their viewing pleasure? Collins tried to clear the matter up: 'They were not particularly intended to be biracial,' she told *Entertainment Weekly*. 'It is a time period where hundreds of years have passed from now. There's been a lot of ethnic mixing. But I think I describe them as having dark hair, grey eyes, and sort of olive skin. You know, we have hair and make-up. But then there are some characters in the book who are more specifically described.'

As Rowling and Meyer had found when the casting had taken place for the *Harry Potter* and *Twilight* movies, Collins and the team were discovering that transferring a fiercely popular young adult novel series to the big screen comes with excess baggage. Some of the book's fans have hugely passionate beliefs over who and what the characters are. Feelings ran so high that the whole process must have felt not unlike treading on eggshells for the film-makers. Director Gary Ross, speaking to *Entertainment Weekly*, defended the casting of all the movie roles. 'It's wonderful that people have such a vivid image of Katniss and Peeta and Gale and they hold it so dearly,' he said. 'But Suzanne [Collins] and I have the advantage of having seen these guys audition for these roles, and I would never judge any role or any actor until I've seen them perform it.'

The cast had their work cut out to perform their respective roles. As for preparing her physique for the part of Katniss, Jennifer felt a heavy sense of responsibility. As a role model for a generation of girls, she was keen to not promote an overly skinny image. 'I'm never going to starve myself for a part . . . I don't want little girls to be like, "Oh, I want to look like Katniss, so I'm going to skip dinner,"' she told *Elle* magazine. 'That's something I was really conscious of during training, when you're trying to get your body to look exactly right. I was trying to get my body to look fit and strong – not thin and underfed.' Josh was encouraged to 'buff up' for the film, with the crew wanting him to slap on fifteen pounds of muscle. As he told Collider: 'It was cool to go through that sort of physical transformation.' Meanwhile Liam was told to lose a little bit of weight – 'I wanted to look hungry,' he said. Jennifer also worked hard with the bow and arrow – so much so that perceptions spread that she was now at an Olympic level. 'I do love archery,' she told *W* magazine. 'I could kill someone with a bow and arrow if they'd hold still!'

As well as Jennifer dying her hair, there were other physical tweaks to make to the actors for the film. Josh, for instance, had his hair bleached several times to lighten it. Linda Flowers admits that she feared Josh would not be able get his hair to the right tone. 'But I think bleaching the eyebrows and doing different tones of blonds in the hair really worked. I mean, like, Josh is Peeta. He's everything Peeta is.' Flowers also made further changes to Jennifer's hair, staying with the 'signature braid' like the book. She admitted that creating a braid that is 'interesting' and 'like something that someone might wear in the future' was a 'challenge'. Ve Neill said that she tried to keep Jennifer as 'youthful as possible'.

All this attentiveness and hard work was essential; this was not to be an easy film and its making was no place for lazy talent. Viewers would need to believe that the Katniss on the big screen could win *The Hunger Games*. While cinematic effects can contribute to such perceptions, the crew wanted Jennifer's abilities to be as natural as possible. They set her on a tough regime of running, with a coach putting her through her paces, and stunt training. She also had to learn to sing, with help from T Bone Burnett, a twelve-time Grammy Award-winning musician. There was an element of overall physical reinvention in her preparations. Jennifer was approaching action hero stature for the part of Katniss, an all-singing and all-fighting icon.

Jennifer's profile rocketed the moment she was unveiled as the lead character for the movies. She soon became synonymous with hilarious, honest and occasionally bizarre interviews. It was as if she could not help herself but say shocking things. 'I did this to *The New York Times*,' she told *Entertainment Weekly*. 'My publicist called me and was like, "This is the *New York Times*, be serious." And then I found myself talking about orgies in three seconds.' Jennifer was adjusting to a whole new level of fame. With it came the increased danger that she would be misrepresented in the press. Just such an incident came when she was, she believes, misquoted about the star of *Twilight*, Kristen Stewart. With *The Hunger Games* already being marked down in the media as a bitter rival of the vampire series, and with the added dimension of Jennifer's unsuccessful audition for the part Stewart took, this story was in danger of spreading like wildfire. Jennifer moved quickly to clear up the confusion. As she explained later to *Access Hollywood*: 'She wrote me back, and she was like, "It's fine. Welcome to the world where everything you say gets turned into [something it's not]." So, she understood.'

Before Jennifer, Josh and Liam knew it, it was time to make the film, which was mostly shot in North Carolina, in 'beautiful, beautiful forests', as Liam put it. Filming began on 23 May 2011. It would take the best part of five months to shoot – five hot, sticky and tiring North Carolina summer months. Jennifer commented that her *Games* costume seemed so perfect when she wore it in the fitting – but in the North Carolina heat it was, she said, quite different. Summers in that region can be wet, too. The summer of 2011 was one such summer. During a tough scene the skies opened up and filming had to be abandoned. Other perils included bears and wild turkeys. The latter creatures would often disrupt filming; thankfully, bears were less prominent. Nobody wanted to play any sort of game with a hungry bear.

Gary Ross felt that a central challenge was to 'convey the immediacy, the first-person point of view the book has'. So he kept to the point of view of Katniss wherever possible. He wanted, he said, to put cinema-goers right into Jennifer's shoes. She and her two key co-stars bonded quickly, said Jennifer, and coped with the pressure of it all by being playfully immature. 'Josh and Liam are really great friends too,' she told *Seventeen*. 'They are hilarious and sweet. They are like my brothers. As soon as we all got together, we reverted back to being thirteen-year-olds. Josh and I were neighbours and every time I would come in late I would go bang on the door and wake him up and we'd all hang out.'

Trust Jennifer to be ringmaster. Sometimes, she was playful to the point of immaturity and boisterous to the point of loutishness. Telling an *Entertainment Weekly* interviewer that she finds farts 'hilarious', she said that an occasional on-set game of hers was to fart into her cupped hands, and then 'throw' the smell into the face of a fellow cast or crew member, shouting: 'Take a bite out of that cheeseburger!' She not only initiated the pranks – she was on the receiving end of some, too. For instance, Josh played a prank directly on Jennifer one day. As he recalled to *OK!* magazine, he found a dummy on set, 'a really gnarled-up, scary-looking thing', and left it in the bathroom in his co-star's trailer. Jennifer was so scared when she found it that, she told Josh, she 'actually peed her pants'. He laughed at her response but immediately began to fear that she might exact revenge upon him. 'I'm just terrified because she's someone I can see taking it to the next level, and somebody could get hurt,' he told The Edge.

This was not a film set for shrinking violets. Indeed, during some play-fighting one day, Josh was accidentally knocked unconscious by Jennifer. A kick she unleashed was not supposed to hit Josh but it did, with dramatic consequences. 'We were just goofing around, and like doing some shadow boxing for fun,' Hutcherson told the *Late Show with David Letterman*. 'She throws this beautiful kick, but it landed right on my temple and literally knocked me to the ground. I was down. I was seeing stars and she was freaking out, crying.' However, it was only the following day that he realized quite what an impact the injury had made. 'I didn't want to make a big deal about it,' he went on. 'But the next day somebody asked me for my address and I started telling them my address from when I was nine years old. That's when I was like, "This is not right." Jennifer felt terrible about it, but it was kind of hilarious.'

Despite this, Jennifer became closer with Josh off-camera than their respective characters become on-camera. 'Josh is so charming,' she told *Entertainment Weekly*. 'And when you read the books about Peeta being able to manipulate anybody . . . I mean, Josh could get – well; I don't know a metaphor . . . except for dirty ones. But he's charming, he's sweet, he's down to earth, he's normal. He embodies all of it and brings it all to Peeta . . . he's got all these great qualities and every single one of them comes across in every line he says out loud as Peeta.' With the saccharine praise out of the way, the pair could continue to trade banter and plot more pranks to play on one another.

When she met the film's senior star, Donald

Sutherland, her behaviour was, appropriately, more graceful. As they spoke, he was amazed she had never read the Leo Tolstoy novel *Anna Karenina*. He gave her a copy on set; she was quickly enthralled and influenced by it. 'And do you know what?' she told *Vogue* magazine later, 'I feel like a pretentious prick for saying it, but it really is my favourite book. Like that quote that goes, "Respect fills the empty place where love should be"? If I had a Myspace, I'd do that as my ad. Do they even have Myspace any more, though? I'm getting sooo tired of the world advancing before I'm ready. Like, all of a sudden, no more CDs! And there I was thinking I was ahead of the game with my little CD binder . . .' (Good old Jennifer – ever ready to take the conversation off into a whole new direction.)

As for Sutherland, he was mightily impressed by Jennifer's acting (and less inclined to wander charmingly off the point during interviews). He called her a 'wonder' and akin to Laurence Olivier. Praise indeed from anyone; coming from the legendary Sutherland this was immense. Other cast members offered their own fulsome tributes to the leading actress. 'Jennifer is extraordinary,' Stanley Tucci told *Vogue*. 'She's one of the few people her age who has that sort of maturity without being cynical. She's also got this amazing sense of technique without sacrificing any spontaneity.

I mean that takes most of us fifty years to learn!' Jennifer dismissed all the praise, telling *Vogue*: 'Me, I'm just like this idiot girl who doesn't even know what she's doing.' Her defence mechanisms were as strong as they had been when she awaited her first Oscars ceremony.

But Jennifer continued to impress the assembled cast. Lenny Kravitz, the flamboyant actor turned rock star who played Cinna, was no stranger to the actress, as his daughter Zoë had appeared alongside her in *X-Men: First Class*. While that film was being shot in London, Jennifer and Zoe sometimes hopped across the channel to spend some time at Lenny's Paris home. He and Jennifer became, he said, 'friendly' during those visits. 'She's really sweet,' he told CNN. When he subsequently saw her act in *Winter's Bone*, he was mightily impressed. 'Wow,' he thought, 'this girl is for real'. Upon acting alongside her in the making of *The Hunger Games*, he became even more in awe of her.

The shooting schedule was tough, appropriately enough for a storyline that involved such draining challenges. Josh described the day-to-day demands as 'crazy', adding that they were shooting three to four pages of the screenplay each day. 'Which doesn't sound like much, but when you realize how many shots you have to have for each one of those things, it's an incredible amount.' Yet there was also a great deal of fun. Josh would put on barbecues for the cast on Saturday evenings. Jennifer celebrated her twenty-first birthday during the shooting. The milestone anniversary was duly noted. Alli Shearmur gave Jennifer the collected works of author J. D. Salinger. There were also basketball games, which helped everyone grow closer. Indeed, as Josh commented, everyone got on so well that it became all the trickier to film the fighting scenes. 'It's kind of a weird transition when they say "Action!" and suddenly there's a giant bloodbath,' he told the official *Hunger Games* book.

One way or another, it seems the filming of the reaping scenes was what stood out for many of the cast. Liam told MTV it was probably the hardest of the scenes to shoot. 'The reaping stuff that we shot was pretty hard,' he said. 'I remember turning up to set the first day and looking out at the few hundred extras there – it looked like a prison camp. It looked so rough and really did look how I think it would be, and it was hot. It was some of the hottest weather I've ever shot in. We had extras collapsing because it was so hot out there. That was probably the hardest stuff to shoot for sure.'

Yet the extras were dedicated enough to have read the novels prior to filming, even though this had not been compulsory. During the filming of the reaping scene, director Ross spoke to the assembled 500 and asked how many of them had read the books. Every one of them raised their hands. Ross thanked them and told them: 'You are not extras, you are all actors. I appreciate your work so much,' he said. As Josh reflected later, had he been at their stage of the industry he would have had 'such a great feeling' hearing those words from Ross. 'I mean, I loved Gary already, but it made me fall further in love with him,' he said.

'We had a pretty small crew for being such a giant movie, which was really nice, so when you had these big emotional scenes on set, it's not like there's 150 people standing there staring at you,' Josh said. He had noted that some fans would divide themselves along strictly partisan lines: they were either Team Peeta or Team Gale. While this was not enough of a trend to rival the intensity of Team Edward and Team Jacob in *Twilight*, there was enough of it afoot for Josh to notice it. 'Oh, boy, I've seen a little bit of that already so I'm sure it's going to happen,' he told the Den of Geek website. 'It's funny, though, because they want to make out that it's about rivalry between Peeta and Gale but it's really not.'

Jennifer, too, was a confirmed fan of Ross. She told Collider that she caught onto his vision 'very quickly'. She added: 'Once he got a camera and once he started mapping out his shots and what he wanted to do, that's when I realized he was making a war movie. It was amazing to see it just get better and better.' Liam had been a fan of Ross since he watched his film *Pleasantville*. 'He's a great director to work with because he's very open and very manic on set,' Liam told Collider. 'He tries everything possible and makes sure he gets it from every different angle. He's just a good, energetic guy who keeps everyone on their toes, and keeps the set alive.'

Another man who stood out enormously during the making of *The Hunger Games* was its star Woody Harrelson. Born in 1961, Harrelson became famous first for his role as the bartender on the hit US series *Cheers*. He went on to star in films including *Natural Born Killers*, *The People vs Larry Flynt*, *No Country for Old Men* and *Seven Pounds*. He has won Academy Award nominations and legions of fans, including Josh. 'Woody is amazing!' Josh enthused during an interview with Collider. 'He's so great. He's one of those guys where, sometimes when he's talking to you, you're not sure if he's on earth or not. But then, you actually listen to what he's saying and you're like, "Oh, Jesus, he's actually extremely smart and intelligent and very perceptive, and really gets a lot of things." He's an amazing guy.'

Jennifer feels the same about Harrelson. She

told *Vanity Fair* of Woody: 'We're very similar. He always makes fun of me, because I show up on set and I have no idea what we're doing or even if I have a line. So he'll text me in the morning: "Do you have any idea what we're doing? No? O.K., let me tell you." And last year Woody goes, "Man! I've never worked with somebody who makes me feel like I'm workin' too hard!"' Still in her early twenties, Jennifer already had a list of glittering co-stars on her CV. She could add Harrelson to De Niro, Cooper and other top names.

The cast and crew became so close amid the heat on set in North Carolina that on the final day of filming, there were many tears. This was not just the standard, movie-world theatrics. Ross said the emotion was greater than he had experienced on any of the other movies he had ever directed. 'There was a strange feeling of catharsis and conclusion,' he said in the official book of the movie. 'It was very emotional for everyone. Maybe it was the extremity of what we had done – torrential rains, filming 100 feet up in the trees, lighting the woods on fire, etc. Maybe it was the story itself, but it was a very special time.'

The director spoke for all involved in the film. It had been a harrowing, bonding and satisfying experience all at once. They felt confident they had produced a film that did justice to Suzanne

Collins's novels and that stood the chance of becoming more than a movie – a cinematic 'event'. Here, it seemed, was the sort of film that Jennifer, Liam and Josh had dreamt of becoming part of – one that spoke to a generation and defined an era in human history. These aims seemed grandiose, yet a powerful whirlwind of energy had been created during the making of *The Hunger Games*. Even veterans of the industry among the cast and crew felt that something special had been forged. They all left the production already looking forward to reconvening for the sequel.

Josh, summing up the experience and what he took from it, was no less emotional and gushing. 'Every experience on this film was so much fun,' he told Collider. 'For me, it's great to see a movie that has such an intense subject and an intense dramatic storyline that can still be done in a fun way. We had such a good time on set. Working with amazing people, you continue to learn and develop yourself, as an actor and as a person. As much as I learned about myself as an actor, I learned even more as a person, just working with great people, like Jennifer [Lawrence] and Woody [Harrelson] and Lenny [Kravitz], and everybody. They were just really good human beings. It was just a great experience.'

The lives of Jennifer, Liam and Josh had already

changed in so many ways since they were first cast for the film. Yet once it was released, they would have to adapt to new levels of fame and recognition. Each of the three had been in the public eye for several years. They were also savvy enough to understand that being part of a franchise as big as *The Hunger Games* meant dizzying new heights. Jennifer, in particular, had been prepared for that from the moment she first signed up for the series. Yet even she would be taken aback by what happened to her as the world fell in love with the film.

Chapter Eight

GLOBAL
SUCCESS

The Los Angeles premiere for *The Hunger Games* was held in March 2012. The cast and crew were joined by other celebrities and talent, together with the customary army of ravenous photographers and television crews. There was the standard premiere atmosphere – an excitable blend of enthusiasm, nerves, pride, insecurity and ego. A succession of cars pulled up, and as each of their doors opened a pair of expensive shoes would swing out, heralding the arrival of another star. Some view these evenings as glittering events, heady with energy and glamour. Others see them as little more than a circus. It is hard, if you have interest in movies and the folk who populate them, not to be swept up by the buzz.

Appropriately, it was the film's leading lady Jennifer who stole the show on the night. She was quite literally the golden girl, arriving at the black carpet dressed in a shimmering metallic gold gown designed by Prabal Gurung. Her entrance sparked a whole new level of excitement and flash-bulb popping. Then, it was time for her to work the crowd and the reporters. Speaking to Yahoo! Movies at the launch, she described her initial misgivings over whether to take the part. She managed to add a characteristic on-the-bright-side thought, too, saying, 'I'm glad I took the role but I was absolutely right about the privacy. It infuriates me but I've got to realize this is my new life.' Speaking about those who had treated her differently since she became famous, she added: 'That's always the nice thing, that all the people who used to ignore me are now kissing my ass.' There was plenty such activity on the night: an army of flunkies were on hand to make sure the movie's top stars never let their wide grins drop.

Donald Sutherland singled out Jennifer's contribution to the film for praise on the night. 'I think it's absolutely fantastic,' he told reporters. 'It's brilliant. Jennifer is breathtaking. She's as good an actor as anyone.' She proved a good sport, too, when she saw the funny side of her tumble as she took to the stage at the premiere. She tripped on the considerable train of her gold dress. As director Gary Ross told the *New York Times*, 'She's good at comedy, too.' It was a very Jennifer night out – and her comedy stumble at a high-profile event would not be the last of her career.

Liam was accompanied up the carpet by girlfriend Miley Cyrus. She wore a black beaded bralet with a matching maxi skirt. Referring to her sky-high shoes – and her own lack of natural height – she said: 'They're my highest ones, they're my Liam shoes.' Bursting with pride for her man, Cyrus added: 'I think it's just so amazing to have all these fans out here and see how excited they are for him and how excited I am for him. I'm really excited. I think just to always remember who was there for you before any of this mattered, I think that is really important.' As if to rubber-stamp the sincerity of her family statement, Cyrus's mother Tish and sister Brandi joined her at the event.

Liam had been given advice on his outfit for the night by a man called Paris. Without him, said the Australian, he would be lost as to what to wear to such occasions. 'I grew up in wetsuits and jeans and I'm in flip-flops most of the time, so it's nice to have someone to show me what to do,' he told *GQ*. The towering Aussie was, perhaps consciously, speaking like a true outback dude. There was a part of him, a part rooted firmly in his childhood, which encouraged Liam to never quite settle in the world of Hollywood and all its conventions.

Josh, meanwhile, was slightly more comfortable in this context, partly because he had been through it so many times and from such a young age. He was asked as he arrived at the premiere how he had felt when he had discovered he got the part. He said: 'I was speechless. Words literally wouldn't come out. I literally wanted this more than anything I've wanted in my whole life. The books mean the world to me.'

Then it was all inside for the screening itself – the ostensible reason for the evening. Premiere audiences are often dominated by people who consider themselves too cool to show any pleasure in the film itself. Indeed, it is commonplace for some guests to quietly slip out of the back door of the cinema shortly after their red carpet arrival. This premiere was different. As the lights dimmed and the film began, there were screams of excitement inside the auditorium. Following the showing, there was an 'after party' on the roof of the LA Live entertainment complex in downtown Los Angeles. The catering was by Wolfgang Puck, the music was loud and the networking relentless. Noting the choice of caterer, according to the *New York Times* one guest was heard to remark: 'Doesn't anyone besides Wolfgang Puck cater in L.A.?' As for Jennifer, she had found the entire evening an eye-opener. 'I didn't really realize what it was until I walked the carpet,' she told a reporter late in the evening. Liam would later recall the sheer raw emotion of the evening: 'We had young girls with tears in their eyes,' he told *Glamour*. 'It's exciting to see the passion. It's cool.'

Next up was the first New York screening of the film – an East Coast premiere, of sorts. The passion of the fans was clear again. Jennifer again stood out – quite literally. She wore a green pleated dress with a V-neck so deep that her cleavage was clear to see. At a book signing earlier, her outfit had prompted plenty of discussion. Upon her arrival at the Cinema Society screening that evening it sparked a storm of snapping from the photographers. Jennifer and her outfits became something of a theme at the various launches: at the German premiere she wore a red minidress – again causing much excitement and comment.

With the premiere out of the way, it was time for the movie's full release. The hype had been ferocious for months, but would it be matched by ticket sales? The team nervously awaited the first feedback. So much time, thought, expense and love had been staked on making it work. Just a week previously, a hint of the demand came when four tickets to the premiere had been auctioned at a charity fundraiser at the Santa Monica Civic Auditorium. They had fetched $2,000. Then, in the first day of pre-sales, the film broke all previous ticket buying records, even outselling *Twilight*. Indeed, many industry figures were predicting that *The Hunger Games* would go on to become as popular a franchise as both *Twilight* and *Harry Potter*.

How could it have prompted such optimism during an era in which the combined shadows of economic uncertainty and increased piracy were seeing empty screenings at cinemas across the world? The film's release benefited from a formidable and intricately planned marketing campaign from a twenty-one-person team at Lionsgate. Despite a relatively modest marketing budget of $45 million, the team harnessed the power of social media to awesome effect. The team did pursue, in good number, the more traditional forms of promotion, including giving away 80,000 posters, setting up almost fifty magazine cover stories, and advertising on 3,000 billboards and bus shelters.

However, the heart and soul of the campaign was a twelve-month push to promote the film via online social networks such as Twitter, YouTube, Facebook and Tumblr. Among the gimmicks used were the launch of the films fiery logo to bloggers, Facebook competitions and a 'scavenger hunt' on Twitter. Together with iPhone games and other treats, these social networking efforts were so successful in creating hype and excitement among the online community that the marketing team was soon punching above its comparatively light weight. (Big movie studios often spend over $100 million on marketing and assemble marketing teams of more than 100 people.)

It was an intricately devised plan: Danielle DePalma, the senior vice president of digital marketing, penned a chronology for the entire online campaign, employing spreadsheets which were coded in twelve different colours. They listed what would be introduced on a day-by-day, and even minute-by-minute, basis over twelve months. At the head of the Lionsgate team was the chief marketing officer Tim Palen. Suzanne Collins was a fan of Palen, telling the *New York Times*, 'He's a generous collaborator. His work is so exceptionally good, I rarely had any notes. If he keeps his emails, he must have about fifty from me that say, "That looks amazing!"' The newspaper's Brooks Barnes was also a fan of Palen, praising him and his campaign generously in the *New York Times*'s pages.

As Lionsgate discovered, the hype worked. On its opening weekend in March 2012, *The Hunger Games* played in 4,137 locations, including 268 IMAX theatres. Over the two days, it took in a record $155 million in North America. As well as being thrilling in itself, this set up the tantalizing prospect of what the film could eventually generate. For instance, the previous record holder, *Alice in Wonderland*, directed by Tim Burton, took in $116.1 million over its first three days and went on to surpass $1 billion in ticket sales globally. The fact the film was released in late winter/early spring only added to the significance of its sales figures. 'It proves that distributors don't have to wait until the summer or the holiday season to release tent poles,' editor of Boxoffice.com Phil Contrino told the *New York Times*. ('Tent poles' is an industry term for leading films.) 'If a movie looks intriguing, customers will show up, no matter what the calendar reads,' he added.

Audiences did show up and they loved what they saw – exit polls gave it an A score. All of the data was thrilling, not least the box office takings, of course. Lionsgate chief Joe Drake responded to the news by describing to the *New York Times*, via email, the reaction of the Lionsgate team. 'I'm watching the looks on their faces as the numbers come in and they realize what they've accomplished – the greatest joy in the business!!!' It was a satisfying and thrilling time for the team; their hard work was paying off.

Meanwhile, Jennifer was enduring a tricky weekend. She felt anxious and sick as she thought about the enormity of it all. 'I was really upset the day that *Hunger Games* came out, I was shaking all day wrapped in a blanket,' she told *Vogue* magazine. A friend, presumably just trying to help, reminded

Jennifer of the pressure that celebrities such as pop singer Britney Spears were under. Jennifer recounted the conversation: 'She said, "Dude, have you seen what they've done to Britney Spears, she's standing on a stand and they're, like, poking at her" … It's like, "Thanks, already!"' Jennifer was preoccupied by the fear that she would be built up only to be knocked back down. This was far from being an unfounded or irrational fear: many stars had experienced the cruel hand of the celebrity media.

During that nervous weekend, Jennifer was concerned more about the wider celebrity media as opposed to the movie reviewing community. She felt a sudden attack of vulnerability. Having decided to discard the fears she felt when first offered the part of Katniss, she was now connecting afresh with that anxiety. Yet she was interested to read the reviews – and she had little to worry about. *Empire* magazine said, 'Lawrence is perfect as Katniss, there's very little softness about her, more a melancholy determination that good must be done even if that requires bad things.' The *Hollywood Reporter* took a similar tone, saying that her Katniss came across 'just as one might imagine her from the novel'.

The *New Republic* was one of the few publications to take aim at Jennifer. 'Lawrence has great ability, and the publicity says she got in shape for this adventurous role,' began David Thomson in his subtly titled piece: 'Why I Hate *The Hunger Games*'. He continued: 'Still, she looks as well-fed or un-hungry as a star player on the UCLA water-polo team, and as placid or chlorinated.' Towards the end of his article he aimed his sympathy in Jennifer's direction: 'I grieve for Jennifer Lawrence to think that vital years will be given over to the drivel of this franchise,' he wrote. The *Chicago Sun-Times* felt that the film was 'too long and deliberate as it negotiated the outskirts of its moral issues', though it at least felt that Jennifer was 'strong and convincing'.

The *Evening Standard* said that Josh lacked Jennifer's 'charisma' but 'has a nice line in wounded devotion'. Liam was rarely mentioned in reviews due to his lesser part in the series opener, though, as Digital Spy noted, he would 'figure more heavily in all-but-guaranteed sequels *Catching Fire* and *Mockingjay*'. CNN mentioned the lauded men, concluding that Josh 'quickly establishes a strong, appealing presence', while it felt that Liam 'brings humour and a bruised heart to a boy who needs to mature fast'. On a broader note, Fox News came up with a typically attention-grabbing, slap-it-on-the-poster conclusion, demanding: 'Move over *Harry Potter*. A darker, more mature franchise has come to claim your throne.'

So the audiences and most of the reviewers were giving the film a big thumbs-up, to the delight of all concerned. Of added significance to Collins was how the audiences responded. As she had explained to the *New York Times*, she was curious whether the audiences would see themselves as part of the audience in the film. 'Will you actively be rooting for certain tributes to live or die? Or will you distance yourself from the experience? How much will you be caught up in the Capitol's Game? I can't even answer that question myself yet, but I'm really intrigued by it.' The demographics of the audiences were interesting. Some thirty-nine per cent were male, compared with the *Twilight* films where only twenty per cent were male.

As such, the stars of the film were gaining recognition and popularity among a broader spread of people. Most men had either sneered at *Twilight* or recognized its stars only in a mocking sense. In the case of *The Hunger Games*, men were actively, even proudly, falling in love with the movie and its stars. The paparazzi were quick to note the peak in the stars's bankability. Each of the leading three became an ever more attractive scoop for intrusive photographers. Jennifer spoke to the *Daily Telegraph* about how she was adjusting to her soaring fame. 'You can prepare for it in certain ways,' she told interviewer Will Lawrence. 'I know if I don't want to get followed I have to take a different car and I've learnt not to leave pictures on the Internet. But I do worry that I'm too in your face because of the movie. There are posters of me everywhere and when I see posters of other people everywhere I think they're annoying, no matter what they're like personally or professionally. So I worry that I might start p****** people off.'

She noted that the more she was written about, the more that her figure was referred to. As she had never been, nor wanted to be, a size zero, she was in something of a minority among Hollywood actresses. *Vogue* asked her how she felt about size zero girls, sometimes known as 'lollipops'. She replied: 'Oh God, yes, I'm so tired of the lollipops. I mean, if I looked like that I wouldn't be tired of it, obviously. But it's hilarious, the way I'm supposedly the overweight one? Like, they got me at the movies yesterday and the caption read something like "Curvy star cannot wait to dig into tub of popcorn." I mean, c'mon! I'm just a normal girl who likes to eat! At least they got me using my hands.' She has mixed feelings about her status as a poster girl for fuller figures.

Indeed, she is conflicted over the entire fame game. The more famous she became, the more she seemed to identify the contradictions within it. The praise she was receiving was fulsome, yet to Jennifer there were many people far more remarkable than her in the world. She was very keen to avoid losing perspective and becoming a deluded Hollywood stereotype. 'I just don't get it,' she said of the way some admirers spoke of her. 'I don't feel any cooler for what I do. When I meet somebody who actually does something to help other people, like a doctor or, I don't know, even a financial adviser, that's impressive to me. "You can do math? That's amazing." I'm so aware of all the BS that surrounds Hollywood and how everyone gets on this high horse and thinks that they're curing cancer, and it makes me so uncomfortable.' When some actors make such self-deprecating statements they come across as less than entirely sincere. For many readers, Jennifer's humble sentiments came across as authentic.

While she had been aware of the rush of attention that *The Hunger Games* would bring, the atmosphere on the set had left her somewhat off guard as the hype kicked in. While she and the team knew deep down they were working on what was set to be a massive movie, an atmosphere of intimacy was created that clouded the scale of it all. She said it 'feels like an indie', during a junket interview with Collider. 'Making it felt so un-tentpole, and even watching it I feel that way as well,' she continued. 'I think it's odd to kind of leave the set and leave the creative process that felt so organic and small in so many ways, and then all of a sudden to do this press tour and to find out that it's so much bigger than it felt on set.'

Jennifer, Liam and Josh

It took a little while to adjust to her new stature, but Jennifer soon gained some perspective on the realities of her new existence. 'I call my mom sobbing all the time,' she admitted during an interview with *Vanity Fair*. 'But it's dealing with the repercussions of having no more anonymity. You lose privacy.' She added that there were upsides to fame, including the chance it gave her to cheer the afflicted: 'Children are in the hospital, and just going and meeting them can lift their spirits and give them hope. As much as this is a curse, as stupid as it sounds, to make as much money as I am by doing something that I love, it's hard not to regret it when you're being chased by fifteen strangers. All you want to do is rent a house, but then you have to rent one with a gate, and you're like, "What have I done? This is so stupid."'

In the case of Josh, he too was keen to emphasize that he had not changed as a result of his soaring celebrity. 'I've changed a lot, I wear nothing but high-end designer suits. I fly private everywhere,' he joked in an interview with the *Belfast Telegraph*. On a more serious note, he clarified: 'I haven't changed at all.'

Liam returned in his mind to his roots when speaking about the realities of fame – and he said his status as a pin-up did not sit comfortably with him. He told *US Weekly* he felt 'fortunate' to be part of *The Hunger Games* story and all that came with it, adding: 'I don't consider myself a heartthrob in any way, though. I'm just pinching myself.' He loved the promotional tour the cast undertook to promote the film, telling About.com: 'I mean, the travelling has been crazy. The mall tour was absolute madness. Just seeing all the fans and just seeing how passionate they were, that was definitely a highlight for me.'

Amid all the focus on *The Hunger Games* it was easy to forget that all three stars were continuing to appear in other films, too. Some of these projects had been shot before the trio had signed up for the project, setting up uncomfortable moments. Josh starred in *Detention*. Not only that, he got an executive producer credit for the film, taking him one step closer to the day when he will make his own movie. Naturally, he was excited. 'It was awesome for me,' he told About. com. 'I've grown up on movie sets and wanted to get behind the camera, so to get that opportunity here was awesome.' Describing the film, which is a curious blend of several genres, he name-checked some fine films of old. 'I think it definitely references *The Breakfast Club*, for sure,' he said. 'I think this movie has so many different things happening in it – pretty much every genre that exists. To me, it's like *Back to the Future* mixed with *The Breakfast Club* mixed with *Scream*. Those are kind of three that I feel this movie is represented by.'

This outing also marked his first appearance in a

horror movie. He said he had not been consciously boycotting the genre, it was just that *Detention* was the first such project he was offered which appealed enough for him to take it on. 'I haven't been avoiding the genre, I just don't think the right thing has come along yet,' he said. 'I think that there's never really been a project that I wanted to do that was in the horror genre.' He said he himself has few fears – apart from a pronounced dose of arachnophobia. 'As far as what I'm afraid of, I hate spiders,' he said. 'I'm pretty good at being not afraid of almost anything, except for spiders. They just scare the crap out of me.' He needed to skateboard for the part and his past experiences with the pastime were of use on set. 'I don't really do it much. I can. It apparently helped that I had some skateboarding history for the film,' he said. 'But I definitely stepped it up quite a bit when it came time to film.'

He also appeared in *The Forger*. Josh played his namesake Joshua, a troubled homeless California teenager. In this film, previously titled *Carmel*, his character finishes a painting started by an artist and soon finds himself caught up in a community of art forgers. He starred alongside Lauren Bacall and Hayden Panettiere. He made a briefer outing in *7 Days In Havana*, the Spanish-language anthology film set in the Cuban capital. Here he played a young American actor – 'so it wasn't a whole lot of acting,' he said. 'He meets some girls, sort of, and some guys, so he has a good time,' added Josh. He enjoyed working with director Benicio del Toro, who he described as 'a collaborator' who made him feel 'comfortable'.

Another 2012 release featuring Josh was *Red Dawn*, the American war film directed by Dan Bradley. Also in the cast was Chris Hemsworth, brother of Liam. In *Red Dawn*, Josh and his co-stars portray a group of youths who defend their home town from an invasion by North Korea. It took a beating from the critics. The *Hollywood Reporter* found little nice to say about it, writing that apart from Hemsworth the cast were 'wholly unconvincing in their roles'. The *New York Times* also gave Hemsworth praise amid a generally negative review, though it said that Josh, too, managed to 'escape embarrassment' with a fine performance. The *Los Angeles Times* was not moved to say any more than that it was 'reasonably dopey fun'.

For Josh, the film was a blast from the past when it hit the big screen, as it had been made three years previously. Speaking to HitFix, he described his affection for it. 'It's very action-packed, it's a very exciting movie, and the characters, you really care about them,' he said. 'And to me in a movie, especially in an action film, it's important to have characters you care about, so when you see them

get shot, you see them get hit, you actually [go] …
"oh my god, my character that I like is gonna get
killed!"' The varying pace of the movie world meant
significantly different eras in Josh's career and life in
general were colliding. The actor who appeared in
Red Dawn was still relatively inexperienced and still
in the early stages of ascendancy. The person who
shot that film was a youngster barely out of his mid-
teens. Yet by the time the war film was in cinemas,
the actor was globally famous and self-assured as a
result of *The Hunger Games*, and the person was a
man on the brink of his twenties.

Meanwhile, Jennifer's other main release of 2012
was the horror/thriller film *The House at the End of
the Street*. This was a reminder of the pre-*Hunger
Games* era in which she took part in the film. In
truth, *The House* is not a classic movie by any means,
so it seemed odd that it featured the young actress
who was quickly becoming Hollywood's woman
of the moment. The critics were merciless. *Time Out*
called it 'shockingly uneventful'; the *New York Times*
described it as 'a choppily edited, poorly timed mess';
while *Total Film* said of Jennifer that 'its talented lead
is reduced to being just another scantily clad babe
getting stalked by a psycho'. Although the film was
savaged by some critics, Jennifer managed to avoid
the worst of the fallout. 'Jennifer Lawrence does her
best with a dull and derivative script in this by-the-

numbers suburban shocker,' said *The Guardian*'s Dafyyd Goff. The same article suggested that the film had been released 'without much fanfare', in order to 'limit the damage to her CV'.

Liam belatedly got a part in *The Expendables 2*. As we saw earlier, the initial part he discussed became 'expendable' before he had even shot a scene. However, Liam remained in contact with the film's star Sylvester Stallone, and eventually picked up a different role. 'He brought me back in the second one and called me up and said he had this part and I said, "Absolutely,"' Liam told Collider. He appears among a stellar cast, which includes Jason Statham, Bruce Willis, Jet Li, Dolph Lundgren, Terry Crews and Randy Couture. 'It's been pretty incredible working with all of these guys,' he told Flicks and Bits. 'I watched all of their movies when I was a kid – Sylvester Stallone's movies, *Rocky* and *Rambo*, the *Terminator* movies, *Die Hard* and Bruce Willis's movies, [Jean-Claude] Van Damme's movies,' he said. Of the experience, he added: 'It's pretty weird to be on a set with all of them at once, hanging out and chatting like you're chatting to anybody. But it's awesome, they're honestly just the nicest guys. There wasn't the testosterone or ego you might expect on a set like that. Everyone was so cool and professional.' During the film, he shot a scene which was physically not only demanding – but brutal. 'I got kicked in the chest by Jean-Claude Van Damme which was an honour, I think,' he told *GQ*. Well, at least he was not accidentally knocked unconscious, as Josh had been on *The Hunger Games* set.

In a sense, then, some of these films that were shot prior to *The Hunger Games* but released at the same time as that mammoth were like embarrassing family snaps that the stars might rather forget had ever been taken. That said, Liam has stated that, to him, a film is a film: 'We got into this business to make movies,' he told Collider. 'At the end of the day, regardless of whether you're doing a huge budget film or a small budget film, you still want the film to do well, and have people see it. That's the whole point, isn't it? You want to put some kind of message into your films, and you want people to see it.'

Soon, they were talking up the future of *The Hunger Games*, with Jennifer telling Collider that it felt 'exciting' to be returning to the story. 'Which is weird because I remember signing on to it and thinking, "Well I'll probably have fun on the first one and be miserable for the others," but really I'm excited to get back into training, I'm excited to get everybody back together, that was such a fun movie to shoot,' she added. 'And also, a time where an actor gets to do a character and a story that they really love and look up to and feel so strongly about, that happens maybe once in a lifetime, maybe once every ten years; it doesn't happen a lot and I get to do it once a year, and also with people that I love. I love Josh and Liam and Elizabeth, Lenny, Woody – to get back together with those guys is great.'

By the time they started work on the sequel, the surge in attention and scrutiny the leading trio were receiving would reach new heights. Naturally, there was no part of the existences of Jennifer, Josh and Liam that the salacious media, and the demanding public it serves, were more interested in than their love lives. In adjusting to the spotlight that was turned so sharply on this part of her life, Jennifer was struck by a paradox: 'You don't want your relationship to be in the press,' she told the *Daily Telegraph*, 'but at the same time, and this is only a theory, the more you try and keep it secret, the more the media tries to crack it open.' An additional trend can be added: the more the trio dated other celebrities, the more the media became hungry for gossip.

Chapter Nine

ROMANCE AND INTRIGUE

Laughter, cheesy crisps and mutual perving: according to Jennifer, that is the formula for a successful relationship. This was how she described the way that she and Nicholas Hoult spent their leisure time together. 'He's my favourite person to be around and makes me laugh harder than anybody . . . We can eat Cheetos and watch beach volleyball and we turn into two perverted Homer Simpsons, like, "Oh, she's got a nice ass,"' she told *Elle*. 'I never thought we'd have such different opinions on asses.' For any male readers who stumbled upon a copy of *Elle*, Jennifer must have sounded – and, of course, looked – like perfect girlfriend material at this stage.

Hoult was a pin-up for a legion of teenage and

twenty-something girls thanks to his clean-cut looks, yet Jennifer has described him as someone scarcely interested at all in his own appearance. She told *Vogue*, for instance, that Hoult was blissfully unaware of his good looks and paid little time or attention to his appearance. 'Oh, he really doesn't care . . . like he'll sometimes wear these white tennis shoes with jeans, then tuck his pants into his socks,' she said. 'He has absolutely no idea how good-looking he is . . . I think a lot of women and men hate me because of that.' If he genuinely is unaware of his appearance then it is an ignorance that works in his favour: he was voted as one of *GQ*'s most stylish men under thirty in early 2012.

As for Jennifer's attitude to her own enviable features, she could play down her own beauty happily. During several high-profile magazine interviews she has acted the tomboy, rather than the glamour girl. For instance, during a cover shoot with *Vogue* she told the interviewer she was suffering from a 'pizza hangover'. She explained: 'It's OK, I'm between movies, I can eat. But five slices of deep crust with ranch dressing on the side? What the f*** is the matter with me? I woke up this morning and my face was so bloated I could barely open my eyes. Believe me, normally I'm waaaaaay cuter than this...'

On occasion, the tomboy image she had crafted

seemed to irritate her, too. When *Vogue* asked her whether she considered herself a modern-day Queen Boudicca, her discomfort was palpable. 'Nooo!' she replied. 'I mean, I guess people expect that of me, and if I had to kill something for survival, maybe I would, and yeah, maybe I was a tomboy when I was growing up. But I'm definitely a girl now . . .'

To the outside world, then, Jennifer and Hoult made for a beautiful couple, no matter what their attitude was. As we have seen, the couple began to date early in June 2011. As they grew closer, Jennifer spent an increasing amount of time in the UK with Hoult. Each time she came to the UK to visit him, she fell a little bit more in love with London. 'All these perfect little pubs in every corner where everyone is fine with sitting and hearing and talking,' she told *Vogue*. She felt this was a major contrast to Los Angeles. 'The more I travel, the more I get tired of LA when I get back. I've been to maybe six restaurants in the four years I've lived here.'

In the summer of 2012, she and Hoult were spotted at the Jubilee procession on the River Thames in London. Wearing a camel-coloured bowler hat and a parka in defiance of the soggy weather, she sat on Hoult's shoulders to gain a better view of the flotilla as it passed their position in Chelsea. Over the summer, they were spotted elsewhere in London, including Chinatown and in the audience at a performance of the dinner-party play *Posh*, at the Duke of York theatre. They were very much a London, rather than a Los Angeles, couple.

They say that when one is tired of London one is tired of life – and Jennifer showed no sign of weariness over the capital. Her experiences in London with Hoult only served to increase her fondness for British men and the shops their female counterparts frequent. 'British men have these wonderful manners, and everything they say is funnier just because of the accent,' she told *Glamour* magazine. 'There's this cute "I'm trying to be adorable because I know you're mad at me" accent, and then the drunk accent where all the consonants have vanished.' She added: 'I love the relaxed way British girls dress. I think I dress like one. I like Topshop, Portobello Road and Selfridges – although I always get Selfridges and Waitrose mixed up, which has led to a few disappointing shopping trips.' They also travelled elsewhere in Europe, including to the French Riviera, where they watched the Grand Prix in Monaco.

Although they split in January 2013, within months they were rumoured to be back together. As she shot the sequel for *X-Men*, Jennifer reportedly rekindled her romance with Hoult. 'They started the shoot in April as friends, and then one day they just started kissing,' a source told *US Weekly*. 'One thing led to another and they hooked up. All her old feelings came rushing back. Now they're fully back on.' Multiple sources said they were inseparable on the Montreal set. They were lunching together and Nicholas was spotted taking a stroll around Montreal with Jennifer and her family. Jennifer reportedly told customers during a trip to a local HMV record store that she was 'in love again'.

The interest in Jennifer's love life was rivalled, if not actually surpassed, in intensity by the fascination with Liam's, thanks to his relationship with one of the most popular pop stars of her generation – Miley Cyrus. The turbulent, on/off nature of their love added just the right amount of drama to the mix, ensuring that the media never ran out of fresh angles on the story. When we left them in Chapter Four, the couple had made their first tentative public statements about their relationship. All seemed happy and content in their lives. Then, their status seemed to change every few months. The following is a mere snapshot of a busy timeline of media reports and speculation.

They made their first red carpet appearance together in March 2010 for the premiere of *The Last Song*. By August of the same year, they had reportedly split up for the first time. A month later they seemed to be an item again when they were photographed kissing in her car. The picture became less clear when, following a reported break-up in November, the following month Miley was spotted kissing Avan Jogia at her eighteenth birthday party. In February 2011, she was linked with Josh Bowman, her co-star in the movie *So Undercover*. Yet just two months later, she and Liam had reportedly got back together.

This time, the couple remained together, bringing an end to the on/off speculations. So the journalists' focus changed instead to relentless speculation over whether the couple were engaged or had even secretly married. The first time an engagement was mooted was in July 2011, and by the time Miley joined the Hemsworth family in Costa Rica in December, things were looking very serious between the pair. In March 2012, the engagement rumours soared again. In response, Miley wrote on Twitter that Liam was her boyfriend and no more than that. But in June 2012, they announced their engagement.

It had been a breathless and intense couple of years of media focus on them: yet, between them, Liam and Miley did plenty to keep the gossipmongers on their toes. In June 2012, Liam hinted that they were, in fact, already married. They arrived at the Australians In Film Awards & Benefit Dinner at InterContinental Hotel in Century City looking stunning. Miley wore a black minidress, featuring well-placed cut-outs, with high platform shoes and newly dyed and straightened hair. She looked breathtaking, and Liam was at his dapper best in a sharp suit. But it was a comment Liam made during his speech that really caught the attention of the media.

While he was giving his acceptance speech for Breakthrough Actor, Liam spoke about the movie *The Last Song*. He thanked the film-makers for bringing Miley into his life. 'I was fortunate enough to get called back in and read with my now fiancée, and we read together and fell in love, and now we're married,' he said. As jaws dropped in the audience, Liam then corrected himself, 'Well, not married yet, but we will be.' Miley, sitting in the audience, shouted: 'We will be!' All of this was only ever going to keep the journalists interested in the story, guaranteeing attention for the couple. It is widely assumed that of the two, Cyrus is the more hungry for publicity.

Yet she speaks with convincing affection for Liam and the genuine love she says they share. Talking to *Cosmopolitan* early in 2013, she was asked to rank the parts of her life – both professional and personal – that she was most satisfied with. 'Number one is my relationship with Liam,' she told the glossy monthly while promoting some new material. 'That's what I feel the most confident in because you never know; there's so much hype behind my new record, but it could come out and, worst-case scenario, everyone [expletive] hates it.'

She positively drooled over her man, saying: 'I'll literally look at him and [will] be like "You are hot, dear god!"' However, it was the conclusion of her supporting anecdote which sparked the most interest. She said: 'The other day, I turned on the pool heater and it was steaming, and he walked outside and took off his clothes and jumped in the pool. I was like, "I'm gonna faint – the hottest guy of my life is in a steaming pool. This looks like a *Playgirl* shoot." So I took a photo and made it the background on my phone. My best friend grabbed my phone and was like, "Who's that? He is so hot!" That's my hubby!'

That five-lettered word 'hubby' set tongues wagging instantly. Had the couple secretly wed? Yet in the same interview, Cyrus spoke of a wedding in the future, even discussing what sort of bash she hoped it would be. 'I feel the bigger the wedding, the more it becomes a target for people to ruin . . . I don't know why anyone thinks I'm going to have this huge, extravagant wedding,' she said. 'That is so not what I am.'

Separately, during an interview with *The Ellen DeGeneres Show*, Miley had gone into more detail about what Liam's wedding to her might be like. 'It's a lot of weird detail,' she told the chat show host. 'I don't want to be doing too much and be crazy and forget about the moment of it all. That moment of when he first gets to see me in my dress, and everything all together – it has to be perfect, it has to be like the soundtrack in a movie. [It's] the one day where that movie crap is real, that romance. I've been to probably ten, twenty weddings, and I've seen that real look five, six times. It's rare that people just stop to really look the person in the eye and know that this is your life together.'

More recently, Miley's sister Noah has said that there has been no wedding and there are no plans for one. In August 2013, on the red carpet for the Do Something Awards, Noah told *US Weekly*, 'they're not planning yet'.

Given Cyrus's high profile in the celebrity gossip magazines, and given that she seems comfortable with her status, to what extent will Liam's relationship with her affect his career? Will she direct his choices? She told *Marie Claire* magazine that she believed that any career choices by either of them should very much take the other into account. 'You want to make sure you are making the best decisions for the people you love . . . it's not worth making someone you love unhappy over a [career choice],' she said.

It is interesting to compare the way in which the three *Hunger Games* stars speak about their romantic lives. Liam's formula for a successful relationship? 'Unconditional love,' he said in an interview with *Women's Health* – quite different to the more rough-and-ready imagery offered by Jennifer at the beginning of this chapter. Where she spoke of her relationship in borderline laddish terms, Liam speaks of his and Cyrus's time together in softer tones. 'I love sitting on the couch and watching movies,' he told *Women's Health*. 'I don't know if that's girlie or not. I like getting my feet massaged; I'll get whoever's closest to do it.' He has said that his fiancée has 'such a big heart' and is 'so open'. He added: 'We feel very strongly about each other.'

Given his impressive physique and handsome features, the fact Liam also comes across as a sensitive lover only swelled his appeal with girls. *Hunger Games* folk have made an effort to stress that he is more than a pretty face. Jennifer has, for instance, drooled over Liam's body and soul. She called him 'charming', and added: 'He's just a solid brick of muscle and you look at him and you're like "Oh, okay, great!" But he's got depth and he's interesting and at the same time he's natural and he flows.' *The Hunger Games* director Gary Ross also made pains to promote Liam as more than a mere pin-up. 'On first glance he's such a hunk that it's easy to just sort of ascribe a hunk-like simplicity to him,' Ross told *Entertainment*

Weekly. 'But this is a phenomenally subtle actor.'

Josh's love life has never quite attracted the same level of scrutiny that Liam and Jennifer's have, yet as a star of one of the twenty-first century's biggest films, he has not lacked for intrusion either, as we have seen in his relationship with Vanessa Hudgens, his co-star in *Journey 2: The Mysterious Island*. Josh split with Hudgens, who is four years his senior, in 2011. It is thought that she finds it difficult to be in a long-distance relationship and that their busy, global schedules were a factor in their break-up. Their parting became clear when Hudgens spoke to E! Online, sounding very much like a single girl. She said: 'I think it's really important to love yourself and truly just be happy with yourself and just kind of let the rest of it fall into place.' She added: 'It is fun to go look at cute boys. But at the same time, I like being single. I feel like I have all this time for myself to be able to do these roles.'

Josh then dated Spanish actress Claudia Traisac, who he first met on the set of *Paradise Lost*. They were pictured holding hands in Mendocino Farms, Los Angeles wearing matching outfits: both clad in grey T-shirts paired with casual chequered flannel shirts in blue and red. They looked very cute together. Yet around the same time he also confessed to feelings he experienced for Jennifer while on the set of *The Hunger Games*. 'I'd say there's a natural stirring that happens in your body,' said Hutcherson of his more intimate scenes with the actress. 'If you're in the moment and you're in the scene, then whatever naturally happens is what's supposed to happen,' he added.

He has lent his support to the Straight But Not Narrow campaign, which aims to encourage young heterosexual men to come out in support of their gay peers. He recorded a humorous video message for the campaign, in which he argued that it makes sense for straight men to support their gay friends, as they thin out the competition for girls. In recognition of his contribution to the cause, Josh received an award from the GLAAD. He was the youngest ever recipient. 'Emerging as a leader in a new generation of equality advocates, Josh Hutcherson has consistently used his platform to help young people understand that no one should face discrimination simply because of who they are,' said GLAAD president Herndon Graddick in a statement.

In July 2013, Josh was linked to a scandal when it was claimed that he had shared nude photos and an intimate video of himself via a dating website. Sugarscape alleged that back in 2010 and 2011, he had posed as 'Connor' on the website and posted a photograph of himself naked, as well as a video featuring him pleasuring himself. The story broke shortly after US politician Anthony Weiner was caught in a 'sexting scandal', meaning the media were even more excited about such slip-ups. If the reports about Josh are true, then he would not have been the first famous person to get caught this way. Even his ex-girlfriend Vanessa Hudgens had been exposed in such a scandal. In 2007, the actress was embarrassed when a nude photograph of her circulated online. A rep for the star told celebrity news website TMZ: 'This was a photo which was taken privately. It is a personal matter and it is unfortunate that this has become public.' Just eighteen years of age at the time, Hudgens was also fresh out of the squeaky-clean Disney franchise *High School Musical*. This was a story her wholesome image could scarcely afford. 'I want to apologize to my fans, whose support and trust means the world to me,' she was reported as saying in *Now* magazine. 'I am embarrassed over this situation and regret having ever taken these photos. I am thankful for the support of my family and friends.'

Josh, who does not lack for young ladies more than willing to date him, has opened up about what he looks for in a girl and hinted that fact and fiction have sometimes blurred for him. He admitted during the making of *The Hunger Games* that he had found it easy to play the part of 'lovesick puppy Peeta' who yearns for 'cold-hearted Katniss' because he felt it reflected his own experiences of romantic life. 'I feel like every relationship I get into ends up like that,' he told *Seventeen*. 'I'm someone who can fall in love at the drop of the hat. My parents raised me to be very accepting of other people, so because of that, I feel like I might be overly accepting of girls. If a girl shows any interest, I'm like, "Yes! I love you, you're amazing!"'

Josh and Liam have both become global pin-ups for fans of the *Games*. While at first glance Josh is the cute one and Liam the more hunky one, many fans of each would presumably claim with passion that their man has the other characteristic too. Josh believes that his *Hunger Games* co-star Liam is the more appealing of the two young men. 'Let's be honest, his Australian accent kills it,' he said. 'It's an unfair advantage! I'd give the lady-points straight to Liam. Liam is epic, man.' Yet, in Hollywood style, Liam returns the compliment, painting Josh as a romantically compelling figure. 'Josh is a pretty charismatic dude,' said Liam, 'so he'd probably win. I'm not that good at talking to girls. Honestly, he's persuasive, I listen to him talk a lot and he's smart, he's funny . . . he could convince me to do anything!' Get a room, already, guys!

Chapter Ten

WHAT NEXT?

How must it feel to have Hollywood at your feet? Well, a feeling that comes with the territory is one of financial security. With growing success and influence comes a rise in wealth, and between June 2012 and June 2013, Jennifer Lawrence was the second-highest paid actress in the world, according to *Forbes*. The finance magazine estimates that she earned around $24 million, or £15.6 million during those twelve months. The only actress to earn more was Angelina Jolie, who *Forbes* reckon raked in $33 million, or £21.4 million, despite having not starred in a major film since 2010. As such, it is accurate to say that Jennifer was the wealthiest active actress of the moment. *Twilight*'s Kristen Stewart, meanwhile, fell from the top of the previous year's list into third place, with Jennifer Aniston and Emma Stone in fourth and fifth places respectively.

Yet with fame also comes a feeling of insecurity, particularly in terms of personal safety in the face of a monstrous frenzy of attention. This is the price of notoriety, not just for the stars themselves but also for some of their nearest and dearest. In May, a man was charged following a campaign of stalking and harassment of Jennifer's brother Blaine. The man was alleged to have menaced Blaine with regular phone calls, text messages and emails. He told Blaine that he was a reincarnation of Jesus Christ, sent to protect the young actress and be her 'husband for life'. On one occasion, the man is said to have travelled to Jennifer's Kentucky home town in an attempt to confront her brother, sending him a chilling message which read: 'You got me really upset. When I'm upset, let's see what happens, alright?'

Try as she might to avoid becoming another moaning actress, Jennifer has been spooked by some of what her celebrity has brought to her door. On one occasion, she thought intruders had set foot over her threshold, too. 'I pulled into my garage and I heard men in my house,' she told *Vanity Fair*. 'And I was like, "I'm not letting them take my stuff." I had just gotten back from training, so I had the bow and arrows in the back of my car.' She continued, 'I went to my car and I put this quiver on me and I had my bow and I loaded it and I'm walking up the stairs. And I look, and my patio doors were open, and there were guys working right there, and I was like, "Heyyy, how you doin'?"' Only then did she realize they were scheduled workmen.

When she, Liam and Josh returned to film the *The Hunger Games* sequel *Catching Fire* in autumn 2012, they were considerably different people. Fame had changed them. None of the three was a stranger to celebrity when they had finished shooting the opener, but what had happened since had been a major step up. Indeed, the chance to enter the bubble of the filming was something they welcomed. It felt good to be back, metaphorically speaking, in District 12.

If it sounds a bit like returning to school following a vacation, that is certainly how it felt for many of the cast. The familiarity of it all felt tingly. 'It was incredible because it was like going back to high school,' Jennifer told Collider. 'Normally, when I do a movie, I'm meeting people for the first time, so it was just amazing to be able to have the same group of people. It was so fun. And it's a character that I love, and a story and message that I'm passionate about, so I haven't managed to get bored. That's a pretty hard character to get bored with, though.' For the sequel, Liam had a challenging experience on his hands. 'My character [Gale] gets whipped in this one,' he told *GQ*. 'So I spent a couple of days on my knees getting whipped, which was pretty horrific.' Jennifer had spent several months prior to the filming working out to get her body in Katniss-style shape.

A crucial difference between the first film and the sequel was that Gary Ross was not part of the latter film. He decided to bow out after disagreements over how long he would be allowed to create the film. 'Despite recent speculation in the media, and after difficult but sincere consideration, I have decided not to direct *Catching Fire*,' he said in a statement released to the media. 'As a writer and a director, I simply don't have the time I need to write and prep the movie I would have wanted to make because of the fixed and tight production schedule.' Lionsgate released their own statement saying that they were 'very sorry that Gary Ross has chosen not to direct *Catching Fire*'. He was replaced by Francis Lawrence.

Yet Jennifer said that Ross left a profound legacy. A lesson he had drilled into her during the making of the first film stayed with her in the filming of its sequel. 'I didn't feel like an action star, I didn't feel like a superhero,' she told *Entertainment Weekly*. Ross had told her this was right – because she was, in fact, a hunter. 'I felt like a hunter,' she continued. 'That helped keep it grounded in this reality of "she's good at this not because she's a trained killer but because she's a sixteen-year-old girl who happens to be great with her senses." And still, in this second movie, I'm a hunter.'

The production team had a new set of hurdles, obstacles and challenges to overcome. 'We built a big portion of the Cornucopia in Atlanta,' Francis Lawrence told *Entertainment Weekly* of one of the production challenges. 'It was really cold. Just dealing with water in the low forties, and the rocks, and the narrow spokes that we built, and cold actors was depressing. Some days go slowly, and some days there are mounting logistical issues where you just have to figure out how to solve those problems with platforms and water and wave machines and volcanic rocks.'

Jennifer outlined where her character Katniss was in *Catching Fire*. 'After *The Hunger Games*, Katniss is desperately trying to get her life back,' she told *Metro*. 'She's suffering from post-traumatic stress and everything has changed. Her friends and family don't really know her anymore. And just as she's piecing it together . . . she finds out she has to go back. This girl cannot get a break. It's safe to say she's one of the unluckiest people ever.' As for the actress herself, she had a stroke of misfortune during the making of the film when her ear was injured. 'I had to jump into water jets at one point. One of them went into my ear, making a

'PSHYOOOOV! noise. I'm in pain. 24/7. Help me!' At least she was not knocked unconscious, Josh might have reflected.

With the filming finished, the hype began afresh for the new film. This time, the Lionsgate campaign was different: the film series already had a confirmed fan base, so there was less mystery to the promotions. A brief teaser was released in November 2012, to be in cinemas to coincide with *The Twilight Saga: Breaking Dawn – Part 2*. The first full trailer for the film premiered at the Comic-Con convention in July. Jennifer's geeky side came to the fore again when she spotted actor Jeff Bridges at the event in San Diego. The actor – whose films include *The Last Picture Show*, *Fearless* and *Iron Man* – was being interviewed on camera to promote his film *Seventh Son*, when Jennifer spotted him and, full of excitement, began to approach him. She then lost her nerve and ran off, before composing herself and returning to speak to him. 'Oh my God, I'm like your biggest fan, I'm so sorry,' she said, giving Bridges a hug. 'I'm so sorry for interrupting you, there's cameras everywhere.' Bridges took the episode in good grace and played along as Jennifer conducted an impromptu mini-interview with him. 'What's your favourite movie you've ever done? Who's your favourite character?' she asked. 'Did it rhyme with "the Schmude"?' It was all adorable.

Jennifer, Liam and Josh

Josh arrived in the press zone around the same time – but he was more excited about Jennifer than Bridges. A journalist opportunistically asked him how he felt about his co-star cleaning up at the awards ceremonies. If the reporter were hoping for a jealous strop from Josh, he would have been disappointed by the magnanimous reply. 'It was really amazing,' said Josh. 'I mean, it couldn't happen to a more deserving, nicer, down to earth, truly talented person. 'Cause I feel like sometimes it can be a fluke, and [in this case] it's not a fluke. She's legit. The fact that she can go from doing Academy Award-winning movies to *X-Men* to *Hunger Games*. Just, like, the versatility is inspiring.' Touching words, as the Crushable website put it: 'In the whole wide world, there is nothing better than Josh Hutcherson gushing about how much he enjoys his *Hunger Games* co-star Jennifer Lawrence.'

Jennifer, Liam and Josh then settled down to watch the trailer for *Catching Fire*, alongside 6,000 specially invited *Hunger Games* fans. Commenting on the film's kissing scene, which is included in the trailer, Jennifer was her usual witty self, with a dose of Lawrence grossness thrown in. 'Oh my God, we should have brought the clip with the snot … I'll put it on YouTube or something, you gotta see it … there's all this snot coming out of my nose, and when I go to kiss Josh, it connects with his mouth,' she told them. 'So, yes, it'll be very hot.' As the audience laughed and cringed, Josh added: 'There was a lot of slobber.'

In case the audience had not already been grossed out enough, she then explained just why she loved filming the water-based scenes. 'It was so fun, because Josh and I could just swim in the water, or like, pee any time you want,' she said. 'Anytime you have to pee you can just run right in the water. It was amazing, because the water was really warm, and Hawaii is great. I love working in the water.' It had been a very Jennifer performance. The launch of the trailer onto the Internet caused the usual wildfire of excitement; the marketing team is now adept at such kindling. Lionsgate has also revealed that it will split the third instalment of the series, *Mockingjay*, into two separate movies, releasing the first in November 2014, and the second in November 2015. This echoed the approach taken by film-makers to the final books of the Harry Potter and *Twilight* series, both of which were split into two movies to maximize profits. Francis Lawrence will return to direct the final two movies, which will be filmed back-to-back.

In the wake of the release of the *Catching Fire* trailer, there was good news from Jennifer's camp as it was revealed that she had made *Time* magazine's list of the 100 most influential people in the world.

Among those she rubbed shoulders with on the 2013 instalment of the annual list were Daniel Day-Lewis, Bryan Cranston, Kate Middleton and Barack Obama. Each entry is accompanied by a glowing tribute penned by a pertinent figure. In Jennifer's case, it was written by the actress Jodie Foster. 'You'll remember where you were when you first felt it, how you were stuck to one spot like a small animal considering its end,' wrote Foster under Jennifer's entry in the 'Artists' sub-category. She then explained that 'it' was 'The Jennifer Lawrence Stare' and that it 'cuts a searing swath in your gut'.

Powerful and evocative words. Foster then recalled visiting the editing rooms for *Winter's Bone*. There, she was struck hard by the talents she saw in Jennifer. 'I thought, sure, this girl can act. But, man, this girl can also just be. All of those painful secrets in her face, the feeling that there's some terrible past that's left impossibly angled bone and weariness in its wake.' The Academy Award-winning Foster then turned to Jennifer herself – the person away from the big screen. 'The good news is that Jen, her good-humoured, ballsy, free-spirited alter ego with the husky voice and a propensity for junk food . . . Jen, the spritely tomboy from Kentucky – that Jen's got it together. A hoot. A gem. A gem with a killer stare.'

Jennifer was collecting famous admirers and

friends effortlessly. Also in 2013, she bumped into Barbadian songbird Rihanna at a restaurant during Paris Fashion Week. The singer tweeted a photograph of them together, with the purring caption: 'Bumped into the extraordinary Jennifer Lawrence at dinner! #Paris.' Jennifer was in the city primarily as part of her duties as the face of Dior. She arrived at Christian Dior's Haute Couture show in eye-catching style, her outfit – widely described as 'daring' – exposing her toned stomach to great effect. She rolled up to the event at Les Invalides in a crop top and asymmetrical trousers. Her lacy pink shirt had a blue line running down one side, and the same line was echoed on her baggy trousers. One commentator compared the overall look to a tracksuit. Her oversized black sunglasses finished the look off sharply. 'Jennifer Lawrence shows skin at Paris fashion show,' screamed the headline in *USA Today*.

She could do no wrong and there was no sign of a backlash from the media. Jennifer has, at the time of writing, Hollywood at her feet. 'Everyone wants to work with her, whether it's another actor or actress or a director or a studio,' David Glasser, COO of The Weinstein Company, which distributed *Silver Linings*, told *Entertainment Weekly*. 'I think everybody right now wants to find that great Jennifer Lawrence Project.' The praise just keeps on coming. 'She is the least "diva" leading lady ever. Ever,' producer Nina Jacobson told the same publication. 'She's not spoiled, she's not precious, she's not needy. She's a goofball who is fun and funny. I love bringing stories home from the set because I get to tell my daughter, "Look, here's someone actually worth looking up to."'

In a sense, then, her story mirrors that of her District 12 character. Gary Ross, quoted in the official *Hunger Games* book, said: 'Katniss begins the Games as someone who only fights for her own survival. But she ends the Games as someone who's willing to give her own life for something bigger.' Jennifer, too, had started her career just hoping for a break that would mean she could earn a living as an actor. Quickly, though, she became something bigger. As Jennifer herself stated, in the same publication, of Katniss: 'You have to remember – this is a girl who starts a revolution. This is a girl who changes the world!' The same could yet become true of the actress herself, yet she continues to remorselessly play herself down. She was invited to appear on the legendary acting interview series *Inside the Actors Studio*, but she declined. She thought the host, James Lipton, would 'hate' her. She imagined him asking her what her acting method is, and her disappointing him by replying: 'There is no method.'

In the future, viewers should not expect her to

necessarily only appear in dark dramas. For, as Jennifer pointed out in an interview with Collider, she was initially into far lighter and wittier projects. She was asked what she thought it was that had drawn her towards such grim scripts. 'I don't know,' she replied. 'I would hope that every actor who does a dark, intense movie isn't dark and intense, all the time. I'm not.' She explained that as a child she loved sitcoms such as *The Cosby Show*, and wanted to emulate the comic actress Lucille Ball. 'It wasn't really until I started reading scripts that I started gravitating towards those roles. I was still auditioning for other things, but *The Poker House* was the first job that I got. That was when I felt like I knew what I wanted to do and was passionate about. And I was in a sitcom when I was sixteen. I feel like there are a million different sides to people. I have a serious, intense side, I guess, but I also like to watch *Step Brothers*.'

An intriguing future outing for her will be in *American Hustle*. It has a star-studded cast including her *Silver Linings* co-star Bradley Cooper, Christian Bale, Amy Adams, Jeremy Renner, Jack Houston, Robert De Niro and comedian Louis C.K. Featuring Jersey gangsters and dodgy FBI agents, the film is directed by David O. Russell, who has promised cinema-goers a 'wild world of amazing characters'. It is based loosely on the ABSCAM FBI sting scandal of the late 1970s and early 1980s, which took down a number of corrupt public officials including a United States senator. The seventies haircuts, outfits and facial hair are set to give the film a vivid period feel. Shooting of the film was delayed in April 2013 when the manhunt for the Boston marathon bombing suspects interrupted proceedings.

Jennifer is also set to be directed by David O. Russell a third time in the film *The Ends of the Earth*. A factual love story about a powerful oil tycoon who loses everything after he is caught having an affair, the film is made by The Weinstein Company. David O. Russell explained to the *Hollywood Reporter* why he is so keen on working with the actress. 'Jennifer possesses a self-deprecating humour that made all of the cast and crew feel at ease,' he said. 'She is that kind of person. She is the most dedicated person I know. She is devoted to her family, and they have been the true inspiration for her character and integrity. Her acting is effortless, and she always makes it look easy.' She returned the compliment during a chat with Collider, heaping praise upon the director. 'He can communicate technically and emotionally, and I've seen him tailor himself to whatever an actor needs,' she said. 'Most of my favourite performances from my favourite actors are in his movies.'

The movie's producers Todd Black and Steve

Tisch also sang her praises, telling the same publication: 'Her performance in *Silver Linings* was transcendent and was truly the heart and soul of the film. Jennifer was basically asked to play four personalities – depressed, sexy, romantic and a wild dancer – and did them all brilliantly. After seeing that performance, we knew we had our anchor for *Ends of the Earth*.'

Jennifer is also being tipped for the film adaptation of Jeannette Walls's powerful memoir *Glass Castle*. In the haunting book, Walls recalls her dysfunctional, impoverished upbringing at the hands of her difficult parents. It became a bestseller when it was published in 2005, and Paramount soon snapped up the movie rights. The author was delighted when she learned that Lawrence might portray her on the big screen. 'How about that!' she said, speaking to the *Hollywood Reporter*. 'I wondered, how could someone so gorgeous play some poor-white-trash ragamuffin from West Virginia? Then I read she had been bullied as a kid, and a lightbulb went off: we have more in common than we realize. She's been able to tap into that for these performances as this tough chicky-poo who also has this vulnerability.' Her enthusiasm for Lawrence shows how far-reaching the actress's appeal has become.

And what's next for Liam? The Australian says

he is particularly interested in films that combine more than one theme and that can sit on more than one shelf. 'As an actor, I'm always looking for scripts that I relate to, in some way, and things that are interesting and different,' Liam told Collider. 'If it's combining romance and action, I'm not missing out on anything. I get to do it all. I wanna do as many different emotions as I can. It's a pleasure to be able to do both, in the same film.'

Liam is soon to appear in *Timeless* and *Empire State*. *Timeless*, which is directed by action film guru Phillip Noyce, will see Liam appearing as a man who is haunted by unresolved issues between himself and his late wife. He resolves to use the money his wife left him in her will to build a time-travel device so he can speak to her a final time. Meanwhile, in *Empire State* he appears as an armoured truck security guard suspected of assisting in a robbery of one of their vehicles. Liam was very excited about the project – 'because I love [director] Dito Montiel,' he told Collider. One of Montiel's previous films is a favourite of Liam's: 'I've always liked those types of films, those gritty crime films. I just think they're very interesting and the way he shoots things is fascinating and different. Yeah, that's going to be very cool to shoot.'

Liam will also continue working for good causes, including as an ambassador for the Australian

Children's Foundation. In linking up with this charity, which helps children have a life free of abuse and trauma, he hoped to connect with a family tradition. 'I have the best parents you can have,' he said. 'They have worked in child protection for twenty years and have only ever given me encouragement and support,' he said. 'The world is a scary enough place as it is for children. It is important that home should always be a safe place for them.' His brother Chris is also a representative of the charity. Underpinning all his activity is a hope that he will remain humble and grounded. He can be his own strongest critic. When he was asked what advice he would offer to his younger self, he replied: 'You're not cool at all. Don't think you are, don't try to be. You're just not cool.'

As for Josh, his manifesto is simple. 'I love what I do, and I can't imagine ever wanting to do anything else, except maybe direct,' he said. 'So, as long as I am able to, I want to keep acting. Anything that comes my way, I'm open to it. If it's a good script and everything's right, I'll pursue it.' He added: 'You've got to just keep on trucking and make sure you're always being true to yourself. Which is so funny, because – God bless America! – that's exactly what Peeta would say.' Of the three stars, Josh has the least pressure on him. Jennifer carries the weight of being the *Hunger Games'* standout lead, while Liam must negotiate the perils and benefits of being the other half of media favourite Miley Cyrus. Josh's existence is, comparatively, calmer. This suits him – he has always been a quieter and more mysterious chap.

Meanwhile, Hollywood increasingly adores Jennifer. The year 2013 will for ever be remembered in the industry as the one in which she conquered the awards circuit. After her scarcely concealed nerves and disappointment when she was nominated for an Oscar for *Winter's Bone*, this time she was more assured – and more successful. She collected a clutch of awards and gongs. Yet, in a sense, as significant as her honours haul was the respect she gained during the ceremonies. She was glamorous yet fumbling, confident yet self-effacing. In other words, she was authentic – she was Jennifer.

Her award rush began in January 2013. At the 39th Annual People's Choice Awards in LA, *The Hunger Games* won 'Favourite Movie' and 'Favourite Movie Franchise', while the star herself won 'Favourite Movie Actress' and shared the 'Favourite On-Screen Chemistry' award with co-stars Liam and Josh. On collecting her own trophy she said: 'Oh my God, I've been sweating so much I'm gonna drop it!' She then embarked on a characteristic stream of consciousness about sweat, before checking herself and saying: 'Focus!'

Then, at the Screen Actors Guild Awards ceremony, her Christian Dior dress appeared to split around the thighs as she embraced well-wishers en route to accepting her award. She was suffering with pneumonia at the time, so she needed a slip-up less than ever, but she managed to laugh it off. She told Piers Morgan later: 'My pants fell off. Somebody trips me on the way, I remember that. I'm keepin' it together, keepin' it together . . . and then my pants fall off! Yep! Oh, God.' However, Christian Dior stepped in to insist that what had happened to the garment was part of the 'design of the gown' and that 'there was no malfunction'.

There was a further mishap at the BAFTA Awards when she slipped in her seat at the ceremony. One way or another she was puncturing the pomposity of the awards season – but rather than doing so as an outsider, she was rebelling from the top. Jennifer was conquering Hollywood and doing so on her terms. By being authentic, true influence and leadership followed – a lesson that many stars much older than her have yet to learn.

It was during the peak awards month of February that she landed the biggest gong and suffered the greatest embarrassment. Typically for Jennifer, she managed to add an element of unconventional humour to the occasion. She was up for the Best Actress gong for her part in *Silver Linings*

Playbook. After the huge tension she and her family experienced ahead of her last Oscar nomination for *Winter's Bone*, feelings ran high again this time. She, and they, were a little older and a lot wiser. Then, she had eschewed the advice to only eat lightly before the ceremony, instead woofing down a hearty meal. This time, she did not eat anything and felt 'starving' in the car ride over to the ceremony.

However, she felt more confident as she arrived. The fact she knew more people than the previous time gave her a greater spring in her step on the red carpet. As she explained to the press later, the difference in how she felt was stark: 'So, I would always go to these things and I see all these people like hugging, and like, "Oh, my God, John, how are you?" And I am just like er, er, er. And so, I know more people, and that makes it a lot less awkward' (Oscars.org). Yet she would suffer a highly awkward moment as she walked to the stage to collect her award.

She wore a voluminous strapless Dior Haute Couture gown for the occasion – and it was that garment that prompted the moment of comedy. As the eyes of everyone were focused on her, the newly announced winner of the Best Actress category, she slipped on the stairs leading to the stage. Her *Silver Linings Playbook* co-star Bradley Cooper and *X-Men* co-star Hugh Jackman both rushed to her aid. As Jackman later told *People*: 'I had to help her, poor thing! I didn't know if she could get up.' She referred to the mishap as she began her thank-you speech. 'Thank you so much,' she told them. 'This is nuts. You guys are only standing up because I fell and you feel bad. That was embarrassing.'

Later, she gave a brilliantly kooky interview to the press. Here, she was appropriately irreverent as she charmingly poked fun at the assembled throng of reporters and their sometimes peculiar questions. Many stars would have merely played the game, echoing the fatuous questions with equally fatuous replies. Jennifer wanted to be more real than that. She quipped that the slip had been a deliberate and planned event. 'The fall on the way up to the stage, was that on purpose? Absolutely,' she said. She was then asked what had happened. She gave the question short shrift. 'What do you mean what happened? Look at my dress. I tried to walk up stairs in this dress . . . I think I just stepped on the fabric and they waxed the stairs.'

Then, a journalist asked her how her day of preparation had been. 'Today was so stressful,' she told him. 'There was everybody in, my family got ready at my house. I felt like Steve Martin in *Father of the Bride* with all the furniture being moved around my house.' But it was as she was asked what the 'process' was when she had got ready that her humour warmed up. She appeared cutely confused by the premise of the question. 'I don't know,' she said. 'I just woke up and tried on a dress, and it fit, thank God, and then I took a shower and . . . I don't know what, but that's what I did. And then I got my hair and make-up done, and then I came to the Oscars.' Then, she added that she had downed a quick stiff drink before facing the press, saying: 'I'm sorry. I did a shot before I . . . sorry. Jesus.'

She was asked what had gone through her mind when she stumbled on the stair. 'What went through my mind when I fell down?' she repeated. 'A bad word that I can't say that starts with "F".' She was then told by a journalist that she was 'awfully young to have enjoyed so much success and asked if she was worried about 'peaking too soon'. As if to remind the journalist that she was a person with feelings as well as a star, Jennifer replied: 'Well, now I am!' She then had a slight diva moment when she told the moderator that it seemed journalists were being chosen who would make fun of her. The moderator denied this. On a more serious note, she also told reporters that she hoped the film would help tackle the stigma that surrounds mental illness. 'It's just so bizarre how in this world if you have asthma, you take asthma medicine; if you have diabetes, you take diabetes medicine. If you have to take medication for your mind, there's such a stigma behind it,' she said.

As well as receiving awards, she was asked to present some. After a period out of the public spotlight, Jennifer turned up to the 2013 GLAAD Media Awards in Los Angeles, California. Her black flared minidress with sheer shoulders was eye-catching enough, but most of the attention was on her new hairstyle. Gone were the familiar long locks and in their place was a shorter do, which soon became the talk of the town. *People* magazine's headline was typical: 'Jennifer Lawrence's Haircut: Are You Loving It?'

Her hair stylist, Mark Townsend, told *Harper's Bazaar* how the new look came about. 'Yesterday, Jennifer showed up an hour before call time and as she opened the door she was like, "Mark, I want to cut it all off,"' he said. 'I was like, "What? Are we allowed to do that?" And she said "Of course, it's my hair!"' Her wish was his command, so Townsend went about cutting a shaggy bob, complete with wispy bangs. His effort met with her approval. 'She was super excited. It's the shortest her hair has been her whole life,' he said. 'As I cut, I lost track of how many times she said, "I love it!"' Townsend loved it, too, and felt it was a wise move as the temperatures rose. 'She doesn't have to worry about keeping frizz down,' he said. 'She can just rock her natural texture.'

She certainly rocked the do in style at the GLAAD gala, where, alongside Harvey Weinstein, she presented former US president Bill Clinton with the Advocate for Change award. She suffered from a touch of nerves on the night, and accidentally referred to him as 'President Gill Clinton'. She looked devastated as she made her goof and was heard to say 'Of all the things to mess up – his name!' On receiving the award, Clinton joked about how Jennifer would be too young to remember his time in office. 'I don't know why Harvey made Jennifer do that,' said Clinton. 'She really was like two years old when I became president. I met her backstage and she looked like she was touring the Museum of Natural History. This is what dinosaurs look like!'

Earlier, Jennifer had heaped praise on Weinstein, prompting a humorous exchange with him. 'I just want to say congratulations to Harvey and his wife Georgina on the birth of their new baby boy,' she said. 'If he's anything like his dad, he's going to be relentless, passionate, and just about the best mentor any aspiring actor could have.' Weinstein referred back to her acceptance speech at the Oscars when he replied: 'You can stop kissing up for forgetting to thank me at the Oscars.' Referencing her slip at the Academy Awards, Jennifer said: 'I fell on my face!' As the audience whooped and cheered in recognition of her self-deprecating humour, she feigned offence and said 'That's nothing to cheer for!'

Between her trio of slip-ups and her humorous and human reactions to them, Jennifer had done much to reinforce her humble, down-to-earth image. Some actors approach awards ceremonies with such pomposity and intensity that, even as they are honoured by the industry, they are denting their appeal to everyday viewers. Cinema-goers are increasingly turned off by overconfidence, sickening acceptance speeches or choreographed moments of gratitude and false modesty. To see Jennifer, a young lady barely able to believe her success, slipping over at successive events was enough in itself to warm the hearts of the public. Add to the equation her own amusement at the comedy slips and she was winning them all over. More experienced and successful thespians will have looked on aghast at how their polished, considered images were being outclassed by this spontaneous young woman who had kept her feet firmly on the ground, metaphorically if not always literally. Liam confirms this, saying that Jennifer is just the same girl she was before she won the Oscar. 'She's great, you wouldn't even know [she'd won],' he told *Good Morning America*. He went on: 'Nothing has gone to her head over the last few years. When I first met her she was full of life and brings such a great energy to set,' he explained. 'When you're shooting the tough stuff like the themes in *Hunger Games* it can be a little dark, and she's got that great energy about her and she's still that way.'

These are thrilling times for Jennifer. Her stubborn determination to make it as an actress back when she and her mother moved to Los Angeles has paid off. All she was initially looking for was that one break which would make all the family tensions over the move worthwhile. She hoped that such a break might lead to more, but could she ever have dared to dream how much more was waiting for her? What a crazy few years it has been for her. As Jennifer put it to *W* magazine: 'I've been through a lot. I mean, I've been nude and painted blue! Truthfully, a lot has happened in a short time.'

Hollywood loves her and other stars are chomping at the bit to appear alongside her in future productions. Likewise, she has her own wish list. Among the actors and actresses she rates are Charlize Theron, Jim Carrey, Will Ferrell and George Clooney. 'I also like Hilary Swank because she's a hardworking actress, and her story is so similar to mine,' she told Alabama.com. 'Aside from the housing situation, our stories are alike, because one day her mother just went with her to Hollywood, and she just started acting. And I just love that; when you earn it and you're not just born into it. Like my dad isn't a director getting me parts. I just auditioned and I did it.'

Alhough she has made noises about being interested in directing, of the three stars it is Josh who is most likely to take that route. Jennifer is most alive when in front of the camera. Given her clear-eyed, no-nonsense approach to everything in her life, it is very unlikely that she will stray far from what she does best. Having a well-paid job that you would happily perform for free is a precious gift. 'Acting is something that makes me happier than ever, so if I could do this for the rest of my life, I'd be the happiest person on the planet,' she said. 'In the case where it wouldn't work out I would love to be a nurse practitioner.' Do not expect her to be forced into nursing any time soon.

Bibliography

Edwards, Posy, *Liam Hemsworth: Against All Odds* (Orion, 2012)

Egan, Kate, *The Hunger Games: An Illustrated Companion* (Scholastic, 2012)

Gillespie, David and Warren, Mark, *The Clinton Factor: Communicating with Charisma* (Teach Yourself, 2008)

O'Shea, Mick, *Beyond District 12: The Stars of the Hunger Games* (Plexus, 2012)

Picture Credits

Index

(the initials *CF* refer to *Catching Fire*; *HG* to *The Hunger Games*; LH to Liam Hemsworth; JH to Josh Hutcherson; JL to Jennifer Lawrence)

INDEX

INDEX

INDEX

INDEX